—A GUIDE TO—
HEMINGWAY'S PARIS

Hemingway with Sylvia Beach, at Shakespeare and Company. *(Princeton University Library, Sylvia Beach Collection)*

─── A GUIDE TO ───

HEMINGWAY'S
PARIS

BY JOHN LELAND

With a Foreword by
LOUIS D. RUBIN, JR.

ALGONQUIN BOOKS
OF CHAPEL HILL
─── 1989 ───

Published by
Algonquin Books of Chapel Hill
Post Office Box 2225
Chapel Hill, North Carolina 27515-2225
a division of
Workman Publishing Company, Inc.
708 Broadway
New York, New York 10003

LIBRARY OF CONGRESS CATALOGING-IN-PUBLICATION DATA

Leland, John, 1950–
    A guide to Hemingway's Paris / by John Leland ; with
a foreword by Louis D. Rubin, Jr.
        p.   cm.
    Bibliography: p.
    Includes index.
    ISBN 0-945575-14-9
    1. Hemingway, Ernest, 1899–1961—Homes and
haunts—France—Paris.   2. Authors, American—20th
century—Biography.   3. Literary landmarks—France—
Paris.   4. Paris (France) in literature.   5. Paris
(France)—Intellectual life—20th century.   6. Paris
(France)—Description—1975-   —Guide-books.
I. Title.
PS3515.E37Z6894   1989
813'.52—dc 19
[B]   88-39963
                                                               CIP

FIRST EDITION

Frontispiece photograph: Hemingway with Sylvia Beach,
owner of Shakespeare and Company, on her birthday,
1928. Bandage is from Hemingway's 2:00 A.M. encounter
with a skylight in the bathroom of a café. The inscription
reads: "To Sylvia with love, farewell to face wounds
(from any source!), Ernest Hemingway." *(Princeton
University Library, Sylvia Beach Collection)*

—CONTENTS————————————

For Bee and Isabella

— FOREWORD

Louis D. Rubin, Jr.

It is no secret that we tend to see our world through the eyes of the artists who have revealed it to us. We observe an especially gaudy and pinkish, cloud-strewn evening sky and say immediately that it is a Maxfield Parrish sunset. We view a place or remember a time, and respond in terms of its depiction in literary work. Once my friend Lewis Simpson and I were driving to Greenville, Mississippi, when we came to a bridge over the Yazoo River at Greenwood, with a sign on it reading, *Bridge Being Painted. Stop on Other Side to Have Paint Spots Removed from Your Car.* Of course we thought immediately of Eudora Welty, who had taught us in her fiction how to interpret that experience.

Could any visitor familiar with James Joyce's fiction walk through downtown Dublin, Ireland, and not see Leopold Bloom's world? "Composition of place. Ignatius Loyola, make haste to help me," Stephen Dedalus thinks to himself as he hones his argument in the National Library chapter of *Ulysses*. How well Joyce managed is involuntarily corroborated by the indignant response of the librarian Richard Best when asked to take part in a radio documentary on Joyce's life. "After all, you're a character in *Ulysses*," a BBC representative insisted.

"I am not," declared Best. "I am a living being."

Surely it is not among the lesser literary accomplishments of Ernest Miller Hemingway that for what is now more than a half-century he has been actively instructing generations of readers in how to visit and enjoy Paris, France. Since 1926, when Jake Barnes, in *The Sun Also Rises*, set out for the Café Napolitain to have an *aperitif* with Robert Cohn and watch the evening crowd, Hemingway's Paris has been ours as well. For English-language readers at least, his interpretation of the capital city of France takes precedence over Henry James's, Stendhal's, even Marcel Proust's.

Perhaps this is because he was only and always a visitor there, and gave us, exclusively and passionately, an outsider's view. As Mr. Leland points out in the preface to this guidebook, the only native Frenchman who figures in *The Sun Also Rises* is the prostitute Georgette Hobin, and her role is distinctly minor. All the other characters, whether American, English, or whatever, are outlanders and therefore outsiders. To be "one of us," as Brett Ashley says of Count Mippipopulous, is to be a dweller in a foreign place who cannot and does not wish to return home, and yet is not *at home* in the foreign place, either. Rather, what makes him "one of us" is that he knows, whether philosophically or by instinct, that there can be no "home," in the sense of a place where one can feel civic and emotional allegiance to a rational community. To dwell in Paris, therefore, is to inhabit by choice and conviction a stage setting, clean and well-lighted, in which the senses may be indulged and the attention diverted and kept amused. It is also desirable that one *not* speak the language well enough to think in it, since in order to remain there and enjoy doing so one must stay uncommitted and uninvolved, and be able to *not* think about it.

For whatever reason, the way that Hemingway saw and described Paris in the 1920s has afforded that city a particular kind of glamour, a special aura of attraction, that has sent many a literary young American in search of it. It was Hemingway's Paris that the still-young veterans of World War II went looking for in the late 1940s and early 1950s. And for all the critical talk about the decline of Hemingway's reputation, it draws them still—as the very existence of this useful guidebook demonstrates.

Hemingway was the ideal chronicler of the delights of post-1918 Paris, for a number of reasons. For one, no more skilled interpreter of sensuous experience ever lived or wrote. The Hemingway style that strove to get down to what was elemental, the literary artistry that was designed to cut through what he considered was the massively coated veneer of cerebral abstraction and to restore what was physical and "real," could describe colors and re-create tastes and tactile sensation in unforgettable ways. I defy anyone, for example, to read the account, in *The Sun Also Rises*, of Jake Barnes and Bill Gorton opening and drinking a bottle of wine after a morning of trout-fishing in the Pyrénées, without feeling thirsty. If it proved to have its limitations, as it did in the 1930s and 1940s, the Hemingway way with language was unsurpassed at what it was designed to do.

But there was, and is, more to it than sensuousness. The style, the concentration on what could be seen and felt, was not only a method of description, but a philosophical assertion in its own right, a way of confronting one's experience. "You are all a lost generation," Gertrude Stein is quoted as saying as prelude to *The Sun Also Rises*. And although Hemingway later insisted that the use of that remark as epigraph, and the novel's title and the passage from Ecclesiastes as well, were meant to be taken ironically, both the author and his readers knew that it was more complicated than that. The sensuous language, the evocation of the look and feel of Paris and the joys of wine cellar and cuisine and spectacle and casual pleasuring, were artfully shaped as a way of keeping the post-Versailles world at bay, of insisting that the only tenable approach to experience was to withhold one's participation beyond the sensuous level. The characters who inhabit *The Sun Also Rises* are resolute in their determination to deny any involvement in a world they did not make and cannot understand—either that or, like Robert Cohn, they are not allowed to remain members in good standing.

I stress the word "determination," for that is what it is: not a fact, but an urgent insistence. As they stroll along the boulevards, find seats in the cafés, or otherwise position themselves to take in the Parisian scene, they strive to focus their attention upon what is exterior and outside of them, in order to keep from remembering what they cannot make sense of or do anything about. The sensuous charms of Hemingway's Paris draw considerable allure from the pathos through which they are perceived, a pathos born of youthful disappointment and blighted hopes. The attractions of the City of Light, in short, gain in their intensity because so much of what they represent is privileged indulgence: the delights of sensory experience, with the participants at least temporarily exempted from puritanical guilt because that indulgence is prefaced by an assertion of futility, and made bittersweet in retrospect by the Preacher's reminder that "the wind goeth toward the south, and turneth about unto the north; it whirleth about continually . . ." What it is is neo-Byronic Romanticism. Lambert Strether would have understood very well; so would Henri Beyle.

The historical conditions, we may say in retrospect, were perfect for the ministrations of a great literary artist from elsewhere who could participate without feeling politically accountable, and we are fortunate that one was available and on the scene. Ernest Hemingway arrived in postwar Paris with the imagination and discipline to re-create his situation in language, with the result that a salient time and place exist indelibly for us to enjoy.

What awaits us today out beyond Orly Airdrome is an artistic creation that derives its charm and vigor from the creative interaction between a master stylist's vision and the customs, institutions, and scenes of a historical artifact, a *place*. The milieu was worthy of the writer. What we see when we visit there is a physical and geographic setting that has been imbued with emotion and meaning by virtue of its re-creation on printed pages. Now John Leland has catalogued it for us, so that we can go straight to the scene and miss little or nothing that is still available to us. To read this remarkable guidebook is to want to go there, and the sooner the better.

One of the few things I remember from my undergraduate American literature survey is the teacher's lecture on Ernest Hemingway. Not dates and books, but his description of Hemingway's Paris. For twelve years thereafter I dreamed of browsing in Sylvia Beach's Shakespeare and Company bookstore with Hemingway, James Joyce, and Ezra Pound; of visiting Gertrude Stein's studio filled with modernist masters of art and literature; of leaning on the Dingo bar with Hemingway and F. Scott Fitzgerald; of sipping vermouth cassis and reciting the Bible with John Dos Passos at the Closerie des Lilas; of strolling the swept gravel walks of the Luxembourg Gardens' allées where Stein walked her dog Basket and talked about writing; of shadowboxing with Hemingway in Pound's studio and in the basement of the Three Mountains Press; of watching the *poules* on the boulevard with Jake Barnes; of ordering a *demi* with him at a zinc; of dancing with Brett to accordion music in a *bal musette*; and of feasting with her at a champagne breakfast in the Bois de Boulogne.

Older and better read, I now know expatriate Paris was there long before Hemingway arrived. He went, the critics tell us, at the urging of Sherwood Anderson, his literary mentor. Bearing letters of introduction to expatriates such as James Joyce, Gertrude Stein, and Sylvia Beach, Hemingway and his first wife Hadley reached Paris just before Christmas 1921. He would make it his home, off and on, for the next eight years. Here he would fashion a prose that not only would revolutionize American literature but would also make him rich and famous. His first success, *The Sun Also Rises*, put the expatriates in Montparnasse on the literary map; a generation of Americans grew up imitating the styles of Jake and Brett. Sixty years later, the romantic Paris of *The Sun Also Rises* remains for many of us the real Paris. You can find us, as you could find our parents and grandparents, on the terraces of the Dôme, the Rotonde and the Select, sipping our *cafés noirs*, *demis*, and *pernods*, pretending we are not the tourists that we are. Seduced by the mystique of Hemingway, who among us has not searched the canvases of the impressionists for a key to Hemingway's prose; wandered Montparnasse at night, drunk on wine or Paris herself; listened to music coming from a *boîte* in the Rue de la Montagne Ste. Geneviève; stood on the Pont de la Tournelle gazing with Jake Barnes towards Notre Dame and wished ourselves what we were not? The bittersweet *A Moveable Feast* introduced another generation to the same Paris. That much of this account is fiction, the work of a sullen Hemingway settling accounts with the dead, is beside the point. In cafés off the Place St. Michel, Parisiennes still pout their way into your heart; standing outside Gertrude Stein's studio on the Rue du Fleurus, you remember Hemingway's account of Stein's appropriation of "a lost generation" from a garage mechanic; in the mirror in the toilet at Michaud's, you can still see Hemingway and Fitzgerald measuring their manhood; and early in the morning on a spring day, when the horse chestnuts are lime-green and the air crisp, Marshal Ney's statue on the terrace of the Closerie des Lilas is still a congenial breakfast companion.

For most of my life, I knew this city only as a dream. An unreal city in which I imagined Hemingway and the Lost Generation negotiating narrow, cobbled alleys straight out of Gene Kelly's *An American in Paris*, Quasimodo in the shadows, bereted Frenchmen sipping absinthe at sidewalk cafés, chic French girls stirring drinks with straws under Cinzano umbrellas. The first time I saw the real Paris was in 1984, thanks to a Fulbright grant. And one of the first things I did was make the pilgrimage to Shakespeare and Company. From friends' postcards, I recognized the bookstore's quaint green facade on the Left Bank of the Seine across from Notre Dame. Each year many hundreds of Americans, urged on by memories of Hemingway's novels and teachers' lectures, make the same trek to this landmark that I made.

Yet, in 1984, I could find no guide to Hemingway's Paris. And,

I was to learn, Hemingway never knew the Shakespeare and Co. that I knew and thought he had known.

A student from Texas, making up his own guide by thumbing through *A Moveable Feast,* inspired me to turn to Hemingway himself. With the addresses Hemingway gives in that book and a street guide to Paris, you can find the more famous sites—the Rotonde, Dôme, and Select halfway down the Boulevard du Montparnasse, the Closerie des Lilas at its foot, the apartment over the sawmill and Ezra Pound's studio on the nearby Rue Notre-Dame-des-Champs, Stein's studio on the Rue du Fleurus, the Place de la Contrescarpe and Hemingway's first apartment on the Rue du Cardinal Lemoine, the Luxembourg Gardens, the Tuileries and the Louvre. Searching these out, I discovered what Hemingway knew: that Montparnasse is best seen on foot. I followed Jake Barnes and Bill Gorton through the streets of the Latin Quarter, dreamed with a young Hemingway of an older Paris where wolves roamed and tumbrils rattled. As poor or poorer than the twenties' Hemingway, I sneaked through the lobbies of the Crillon and Ritz, gazed enviously at the rich *fruits du mer* in Prunier's window, nursed for an hour a *demi* at the Deux Magots, and treated myself, as had Hemingway, to Lipp's *cervelas remoulade.*

But the short list of such addresses seemed paltry compared to the longer list of defunct places I had no way of locating. Where was the *bal musette* where Jake and Brett meet in *The Sun Also Rises*; Zelli's where Jake, Brett and the Count dance; the Dingo, where they drink; the taxidermist's Jake and Bill Gorton stumble by? And where were *A Moveable Feast's* Michaud's, La Pêche Miraculeuse, the S bus, and La Petite Chaumière? Asked at the last minute to teach *The Sun Also Rises* to a group of French students in Angers, I found them as curious—and ignorant—as myself about many of the places Hemingway mentions.

So began the search that would form the basis of this book. Most of the old places are gone; those that remain are often expensive and cluttered with Americans. But every one of us who dreams of Paris dreams of a city shaped in large part by Ernest Hemingway. For those through whose visions of the City of Light carouse Jake Barnes and Brett Ashley, this book is written.

The Sun Also Rises and *A Moveable Feast* remain its heart. I have supplemented their references to specific places in and about Paris with places Hemingway mentioned in other novels and in newspaper and magazine articles. Books by and about people who knew Hemingway—Morley Callaghan's *That Summer in Paris*; Janet Flanner's letters and memoires; *The Way It Was*, Harold Loeb's answer to *The Sun Also Rises*; John Dos Passos's *The Best Times*; biographies and letters of F. Scott Fitzgerald, Hemingway, James Joyce, and Archibald MacLeish—often provided additional sites or gave addresses of Hemingway locations from the early years. Mary Walsh Hemingway's *How It Was* and A. E. Hotchner's *Papa Hemingway* were helpful for the post World War II years. I relied heavily upon Carlos Baker's invaluable biography, which lists an incredible number of Hemingway sites; *Ernest Hemingway: A Life Story* was the first comprehensive biography and remains, in my opinion, the basis for all biographies since. Brian Morton's *Americans in Paris* is a handy guide for some Hemingway addresses and those people associated with him. Because Morton seeks to list every notable American who ever visited Paris, his Hemingway entries are understandably limited. Neither Morton nor Baker is much interested in the Paris of Hemingway's fiction. Robert Gajdusek's *Hemingway's Paris* quotes Hemingway and others, but intended as an anthology, it is neither comprehensive nor a guide. It lists only those addresses common to most Hemingway biographies, concentrating on autobiographical rather than fictional addresses.

Combining both Hemingway's life and fiction in this guide, I have tried to be as comprehensive and specific as possible in my entries. Wherever possible, I have visited the places in the guide, attempting to discover how much—if any—they have changed since Hemingway knew them. The places associated with Hemingway—the cafés of the Carrefour Vavin, La Closerie des Lilas, the Ritz—all remember him. Some trade on his name—you can drink in the Hemingway Bar at the Ritz, sit at Hemingway's favorite spot at the Closerie, sleep in his and Hadley's room at the Hôtel d'Angleterre. But he is not remembered fondly by everyone; weary waiters at the Rotonde and Select will tell tourists for the ten thousandth time that, yes, this is where Hemingway came. Many of the lesser known cafés, restaurants, nightclubs and hotels Hemingway knew, having since closed or changed hands, are ignorant of their place in American literary history.

Where Michaud's stood is now a café; no one there had heard of Ernest Hemingway two years ago, and they were indifferent to their toilet's fame. For the French, many places we associate with Hemingway have other, stronger associations. Michaud's suggests food, not phalluses; the now demolished Vélodrome d'Hiver is a somber memorial to the deportation of French Jews; and Montparnasse itself was there long before Hemingway discovered it.

Why did he wind up on the Left Bank of Paris in 1921? He had first planned to take Hadley to the Italy he knew from World War I, but Sherwood Anderson convinced him that Paris was the place to be. And Paris, for writers and artists, meant the Left Bank. The Right Bank's Montmartre had been the Bohemian capital of Paris in the 1890s. But by 1914, the artists had abandoned Montmartre for Montparnasse. Near the Latin Quarter, whose student crowds insured continuous revolutions in taste if not politics, with the École des Beaux Arts nearby, Montparnasse became the cultural capital of Paris. It was in Montparnasse that the cancan first appeared and the polka first took hold in France. Here too were the models for what became Puccini's *La Bohème*.

Douanier Rousseau was among the first to come, followed by Apollinaire and others. They chose the café-restaurant La Closerie des Lilas—which Hemingway would also choose—for their Tuesday soirées. Russian exiles—including Lenin and Trotsky—sat in the Closerie and other cafés and plotted political revolution. Eisenstein, Stravinsky, and others plotted artistic revolutions. Cocteau and Picasso joined them. Montparnasse had become the Muses' mountain.

And Americans by the thousands came back "over there." They had learned firsthand in World War I that Paris was a lot more fun than America. By 1922 when Hemingway returned, we had Prohibition; the French had wine. The dollar was strong; the franc was weak. One dollar got you ten francs at the beginning of the decade and it kept getting better; by the time the 1929 stock-market crash put an end to Paris for Americans, you could get 25 francs for a buck. And income tax returns suggest the average Frenchman pulled in a third of what the average American made. Paris had become *the* international art and literary center; everyone who was anyone found a cheap hotel room on the Left Bank to sleep in and spent his days in the cafés of Montparnasse.

However, the world of *The Sun Also Rises* is not, finally, very

French. After all, Georgette Hobin—a prostitute—is the only really French character in it. Brett Ashley is English, Mike Campbell is Scottish, the Count is Greek, Jake Barnes, Bill Gorton, and Robert Cohn are American. This is indeed an expatriate novel, filled with strangers in a strange land. And the nightclubs, bars, and cafés that fill the book are crammed with anyone but Frenchmen. *Every* place in *The Sun Also Rises* was real. And most of them appear in twenties' tourist guidebooks that warn the reader that these are tourist traps rather than *la France profonde*. This suggests that the young Hemingway, at least, was more a typical tourist than one might think. But as Hemingway came to know Paris and the French, he became less dependent on tourist traps. Indeed, he prided himself on knowing the "real" Paris. Many of his friends recall his taking them to out-of-the-way cafés, to the horse and bike races, to boxing matches. He walked for a while in two worlds, that of American enclaves and that of the French.

That so many places were popular with tourists made them easier to locate. I quote guidebooks upon occasion either to supplement Hemingway's sometimes fleeting references or to provide alternative descriptions. *Baedeker's, Les Guides Bleus, Muirhead,* Bruce Reynolds's 1927 guide *Paris With the Lid Lifted,* and Julian Street's 1929 *Where Paris Dines* were especially helpful. Jean-Emile Bayard's *Le quartier latin, hier et aujourd'hui* and Robert Robert's (pseudonym for Robert Burnand) *Le guide du gourmand à Paris* provided a Gallic point of view. Henri Gault and Christian Millau's various guides over the past twenty years supplement my personal opinion of the places that still remain. For those places that did not make the guidebooks, I found invaluable Didot-Bottin's *Almanache du commerce de Paris*—a city directory that provides yearly business indices by type, street, and owner. Jacques Coussillan's *Dictionnaire historique des Rues de Paris* (published under his pseudonym, Hillairet) locates streets whose names have changed and provides fascinating histories of every street in Paris (although, being French, he seldom mentions American connections).

Hemingway, like Dos Passos, e. e. cummings, and others, came back to France as a war veteran. To some degree, they were no doubt seeking the afterglow of the heady excitement of the war to end all wars. But they were also serious artists, bent on discovering for America a language, subject, and form all her own. Not that all was harmony among the Muses. The expatriate crowd had a clique for every café at the Vavin crossroads in Montparnasse. Hemingway pretended to distinguish the artists from the "artistes" by which café—the Dôme or Rotonde—they favored. And for every judgment he made, there was someone in another camp making the reverse. Portly Gertrude Stein presided over her coterie in a studio crammed with paintings on the Rue du Fleurus, but woe betide the man who, like Ezra Pound, mentioned Joyce's name more than once. Dapper Joyce's Left Bank bastion was Sylvia Beach's Shakespeare and Company on the Rue de l'Odéon; here Beach—who seems to have been a long-suffering saint among proud sinners—loaned and sold books to and by the modern masters—among them Joyce, Yeats, Eliot, Pound, and Hemingway.

Hemingway's Parisian haunts changed with his fortunes. At first a financially strapped—at least compared to other expatriates—newlywed, he opted for the Left Bank. He and Hadley knew the favorite expatriate hangouts there, and he put them all in *The Sun Also Rises*. Hemingway and Jake Barnes's Paris had three centers: the Left Bank, Montmartre, and the area around the Opéra. The Left Bank, especially Montparnasse, was where they lived and socialized during the day and early evening. Most of their restaurants—Lavigne's, Lavenue's, Polidor's—were located here. As were the bars and cafés—the Closerie, Dingo, Dôme, Rotonde, Select—on and off the Boulevard du Montparnasse. Cafés were the center of social life here, along with bars and nightclubs such as the College Inn and the Jockey Club. The Opéra district was where Hemingway and *The Sun Also Rises'* Barnes worked as reporters. Most of the cafés and bars he frequented here—Caves Murae, the Hole in the Wall, the Napolitain, Vetzel's—were newspaper hangouts. The Crillon and Ritz had fancier bars, the Café de la Paix was for tourists and putting on the dog. Montmartre meant nightlife, and many of these places—Florida's, La Petite Chaumière, Zelli's—were popular with tourists as well as expatriates.

After he became rich and famous as "Papa," Hemingway began to shun Montparnasse. With reason. He had angered everyone he put in *The Sun Also Rises* as well as everyone he had left out. Leaving Hadley meant he had to leave friends as well. He and Pauline Pfeiffer lived near the Faubourg St. Germain, and Hemingway tended to gravitate to the cafés in this area—the Deux

Magots, Flore, and Lipp's. Rich enough to afford the best, he came to know the better hotels and restaurants of Paris. By the fifties, he had become a regular at the Ritz and Prunier's.

Because I assume any reader of this book to be something of a Hemingway aficionado, I have not provided a full biography. This book began as a sort of annotation to Hemingway's Paris, and it remains primarily that. In addition to the guide, I have included a bibliography of works consulted, a brief chronology of Hemingway's stays in Paris, and an annotated index of characters and people found in the guide. Readers of literature can use the book to learn more about places they run across in his work or biographies. The curious can read it for its anecdotal value. Tourists in Paris can use it to supplement general guides to the city. The walking tours at the end of the book are suggested for people interested in getting a firsthand feel for what it was like to live in Hemingway's Paris.

This book could not have been written without the help of a number of people. I especially wish to thank: Louis D. Rubin, Jr., who is responsible in more ways than even he knows; my editor Susan Ketchin, who deserves a trip to Paris for having breathed life into a stuffy academic tome; John Gatton, who knows more about Paris than I ever will; Yolanda Warren, for summer afternoons at Princeton; Alan Baragona, who knows more about word processors than I care to; Virginia Military Institute, which provided me money and a computer; my colleagues and students who endured with patience my fanaticism; and Bee, who will always have Paris.

A GUIDE TO
HEMINGWAY'S PARIS

— CHRONOLOGY ——————

The following is a chronology giving Hemingway's trips to Paris mentioned in the guide and tours.

1899	H born.
Summer 1918	19-year-old H first sees Paris; Madeleine is bombed.
December 1921	H and Hadley arrive in Paris and stay until 1923 on Rue du Cardinal Lemoine; meet Stein et al. H a journalist and unknown writer.
January 1924	H, Hadley, and Bumby in Paris together on Rue Notre-Dame-des-Champs until 1926 split; Montparnasse period; writes *SAR*.
1927	H marries Pauline, moves onto Rue Férou and stays until 1928; H becomes Papa; *FTA* begun here.
1929	H, Pauline, and son Patrick in Paris on Rue Férou until 1930; boxes with Callaghan.
Summer 1931	Brief visit to Paris.
Fall 1933	Visits Paris; dines with Joyces prior to African trip (*GHA*).
1937	Visits Paris while covering Spanish Civil War; gives Shakespeare & Co. reading.
1944	Liberation of Paris; at the Ritz with Mary Walsh.
1949	Visits Paris with Mary.
1953	Visits Paris with Mary.
1956	Visits Paris with Mary; discovers *AMF* notebooks.
1961	Suicide in Idaho.

1

GUIDE

This guide contains only those places mentioned by Hemingway or by others in connection with him. Entries are alphabetical, ignoring French articles (la, le, l', etc.). Cafés, café-restaurants, hotels, and restaurants are classed here by the key word in their titles (i.e., Café Select is alphabetized under S; the index includes lists of businesses by kind). Where several apartments are listed under the same tenant name, listings are in chronological order. Wherever possible, I include street numbers, arrondissements, and Métro stops. In instances of conflicting addresses, I have followed French sources (especially Didot-Bottin and Hillairet). Several addresses eluded me, and no doubt I have overlooked others. I invite readers who have addresses other than mine or who know of places I omit, to write me care of the publisher. Sources of literary citations are noted in brackets in the text, by author and page number. Citations of Hemingway's works are listed by title and page number, with titles abbreviated as follows: *SAR* is *The Sun Also Rises*; *AMF* is *A Moveable Feast*; *FTA* is *A Farewell to Arms*; *GHA* is *Green Hills of Africa*; *FBT* is *For Whom The Bell Tolls*. Other abbreviations should be self-explanatory.

1. Café des Amateurs

"The cesspool of the Rue Mouffetard," the Café des Amateurs was around the corner from where the Hemingways lived in 1922–23 [*AMF*, p 3]. Reeking of old wine and older clientele, it had been the haunt of *quartier* drunkards for over a hundred years before Hemingway learned to shun it. Known in the 1800s as Les Caves du Panthéon, it had offered to "*chiffoniers, chanteurs ambulants, et vagobonds*" (ragmen, minstrels, bums, and vagabonds) drinks for ten centimes. Five hundred years before that, its ancestral neighbor, La Maison de la Pomme de Pin, had drawn Rabelais and Villon.

Today La Chope—the Beer Mug—stands where the Café des Amateurs stood the night Jake Barnes and Bill Gorton resisted its siren stench of dirty bodies and *pommes frites* on their drunken stroll through Paris. *Quartier* residents still crowd its terrace tables, looking out on the Place de la Contrescarpe where *clochards*— Parisian bums named after the bells (*les cloches*) that once summoned them to sift market trash for food—sprawl in the shade of trees.

[NOTE: *A Moveable Feast* calls this the Café *des* Amateurs; *The Sun Also Rises*, the Café *aux* Amateurs.]

2. American Club

In what is today a cafeteria, Canadian writer Morley Callaghan decked Hemingway during the summer of 1929 in a boxing match refereed by F. Scott Fitzgerald. Absorbed by the fight, Fitzgerald had let a round go for four rather than three minutes. " 'All right, Scott,' Ernest said savagely, 'if you want to see me getting the shit knocked out of me, just say so. Only don't say you made a mistake,' and he stomped off to the shower room to wipe the blood from his mouth" [Callaghan, p. 214].

Gossip columnists gloated over Papa's supposed first-round knock-out, prompting Fitzgerald to wire Callaghan: "HAVE SEEN STORY IN HERALD TRIBUNE. ERNEST AND I AWAIT YOUR CORRECTION. SCOTT FITZGERALD."

In a letter to his editor Maxwell Perkins, Hemingway blamed "several bottles of white burgundy" at Prunier's and "a couple of whiskeys en route" for his defeat. He did not forgive Fitzgerald until the end of the year, when Harry Crosby's suicide prompted him to do so: "One of my best friends [something of an exaggeration] died two weeks ago and I'll be damned if I'm going to lose you through some bloody squabble. Best to you always—yr. affectionate friend Ernest" [*Letters*, pp. 302, 314].

Callaghan never locates the American Club in his account, but Sara Mayfield says the fight took place in "a gymnasium in Rue de Vaugirard run by a doubtful character named Georges" [Mayfield, p. 137]. Now gone, the former Gymnase George, with branches here and at nearby 19, Rue de Tournon (which still has a Georges Dance Studio and is the house John Paul Jones died in) touted itself as "*le plus beau, le plus grande gymnase de Paris.*"

11, Rue Scribe
3. American Express Company
[9th; Opéra]

Like many Americans, Hemingway used the American Express office as a mailing address. Karl Malden's "don't leave home without it" folks are still here, and the office is still crowded with Americans buying more checks, seeking replacements for those stolen, or looking for letters from home.

Bruce Reynolds, in his idiosyncratic 1927 guide *Paris With the Lid Lifted*, praises Dobes, the "Information Man" of the American Express. "Dobes is Mama, Papa, Big Brother, Big Sister, Guardian, Wet Nurse, Judge, Referee, Umpire, to and for, every American in Paris. They question him, quiz him, confide in him, 'confess' to him, lay bare their whole lives to him. He answers every question—from 'What is a Franc?' to 'Do you really think I should marry?'. . . Go meet him—ask him any damphool question and bang will come the answer" [Reynolds, p. 112].

63, Boulevard Victor Hugo
4. American Hospital   *[Neuilly; terminus, bus 32]*

Hemingway wound up here in March 1928 with nine stitches in his right forehead after he pulled his bathroom skylight in the Rue Férou down on himself at 2:00 A.M. Archibald MacLeish drove him to the hospital, his head wrapped in toilet paper, "a magnificent absorbent which I've now used twice for that purpose in pretty much emergencies," he wrote Perkins [*Letters*, p. 272].

The papers picked up the story, and Ezra Pound wired Hemingway, "Haow the hellsufferin tomcats did you git drunk enough to fall upwards thru the blithering skylight!!!!!!!!!" [Baker, *Ernest Hemingway*, p. 190]. Hemingway claimed he mistook the skylight cord for the toilet's. Drunk or not, he had been out with the MacLeishes until 11:00 P.M.

The photo of a wounded Hemingway outside Sylvia Beach's Shakespeare and Company (see frontispiece) is from this time.

27, Boulevard Malesherbes
5. American Women's Club   *[8th; Madeleine]*

In the 1920s, this storefront housed the American Women's Club, or Paris YWCA, which played the villain in Hemingway's life. Jake Barnes blames their guidebook for filling Madame Lecomte's restaurant with Americans in search of a "quaint" Paris. Ford Madox Ford remembered tangling with them over the *transatlantic review*'s absence of capitals. "It was, of course, taken to be a display of Communism. We were suspected of beheading initial letters as if they had been kings. The American Women's Club in Paris solemnly burned the second number of the *review* in their hall fire, thus giving a head to Mr. Hitler" [Ford, p. 300]. Even their friends mocked the Women's Club; Eric Hawkins of the *Paris Herald* claims one ally called them "the American W.C."—the American water closet [Hawkins, p. 127].

44, Rue Jacob
6. Hôtel d'Angleterre   *[6th; St. Germain des Prés]*

Hemingway and Hadley, his first wife, stayed here upon their arrival in Paris in December 1921. A former British embassy and one-time residence of Washington Irving, the then-named Hôtel d'Angleterre et Jacob was filled with Americans, Hadley recalled. Sherwood Anderson had recommended it to Hemingway, who told his *Toronto Star* readers that, "Our room costs twelve francs a day for two. It is clean, light, well heated, has hot and cold running water and a bathroom on the same floor" [*Dateline*, p. 88]. And its worn carpet was a trap for drunks.

Today's carpet is new, the rooms have private toilets, the hotel has three stars and the Hemingways' room—number 14—costs 690 francs a night. Call ahead; the desk clerk says the room is nearly always booked.

In number 14, Hemingway engaged in his first Paris boxing match—with a reluctant and bespectacled Lewis Galantière. Anderson's friend, he had treated the Hemingways to dinner. Hemingway paid him back by busting his glasses.

7. Anglo-American Press Association   Address Unknown

As correspondent for the *Toronto Star*, Hemingway was a member of this group, whose Wednesday meetings and annual bash he attended. He staggered home at 7:00 A.M. from the November 1924 dinner, he wrote Robert McAlmon, a fellow expatriate. Harold Stearns, an expatriate who appears as Harvey Stone in *The Sun Also Rises*, attended the same dinner, which he remembered as a drunken blur of forgotten lines in a skit the members staged and as a setting for his falling "weepingly and demonstratively in love" with the *chanteuse* who performed that evening [Stearns, pp. 238–39].

                                              33, Avenue Georges Bernanos
8. Bal Bullier   [5th; Port Royal]

Today a monolithic student center squats where this dance hall once stood. But Hemingway remembered with fondness in *A Moveable Feast* the oriental facade that filled the view up Notre-Dame-des-Champs where he lived over the sawmill with Hadley and Bumby. In the Bullier's cavernous interior, Parisians *du monde populaire* danced weekends to polkas played on the accordion. The Bullier was a Left Bank student version of the *bals publics* one associates with the Montmartre of the Gay Nineties. By 1913, *Baedeker's* lamented that these "have almost all lost their originality, and cannot be attended by ladies."

The only trace of the Bullier today is the Café Bullier at 174, Boulevard St. Michel, whose terrace, framed in lime-green iron, recalls another century.

9. Bal de la Montagne Ste. Geneviève, Le Grand

46, Rue de la Montagne Ste. Geneviève *[5th; Cardinal Lemoine]*

Now an Italian restaurant, La Montagne advertised itself in 1967 as "*La Plus Vielle Musette de Paris.*" Here Brett Ashley appeared to Jake Barnes's disgust with "a crowd of young men, some in jerseys and some in their shirt-sleeves. . . . I know they are supposed to be amusing, and you should be tolerant, but I wanted to swing on one, any one, anything to shatter that superior, simpering composure" [*SAR*, p. 20].

A celebrated gay *bal musette*, La Montagne was famed for its *Cage aux Folles* proprietors, whose indifference to one's sexual preferences made their place popular with all comers-on. Popular too was Brett Ashley's model, Lady Duff Twysden, whom Hemingway suggested Harold Loeb—model for *The Sun Also Rises'* Robert Cohn—meet at Pamplona with "a band of local fairies at the train carrying a daisy chain so that the transition from the Quarter will not be too sudden" [*Selected Letters*, June 21, 1925]. Jealous Jake resented that he wanted Brett but couldn't have her; Hemingway pursued her model Duff, but couldn't keep her, losing her to Loeb.

A photograph of La Montagne's gay band playing in its loggia appears in Brassai's *The Secret Paris of the Thirties*.

10. Bal du Printemps

74, Rue du Cardinal Lemoine *[5th; Monge]*

This noisy *bal musette* occupied the ground floor of the Hemingway's first Paris apartment. Hemingway and Hadley resented its noise, but danced there. Its current successor, Le Rayon Vert Disco, has a garish green-and-black exterior that may repel the tourist, but the Hemingways thought its ancestor a slice of the "real workman's France." Hardly Les Folies, the Printemps was not nearly as dangerous as the *bal musette* Hemingway painted for his *Star* readers. For them, it became a hangout for *apaches* (French gangs), for whom an evening often as not ended in violence and "a guillotine" [*Dateline*, p. 118].

The expatriate crowd took to hanging out at the Printemps;

in *A Moveable Feast*, a bored Hemingway listens to Ford Madox Ford's plans for weekly soirées there. These weekly excursions into *la France profonde* served as a basis for *The Sun Also Rises*' dancing party that the Braddocks threw. Thrilled with their slumming, the expatriates nicknamed the Printemps the "Bucket of Blood" [Laney, p. 163]. Rough it may have been, but scarcely sinister. Its owner, M. Ribeyre, was by day a taxi driver.

11. Barney, Natalie   20, Rue Jacob
[apartment]   *[6th; St. Germain des Prés]*

The "popess of Lesbos," Natalie Barney lived in a pavilion at the end of the courtyard here. She came under attack in *A Moveable Feast* as "a rich American woman and patroness of the arts" whose salon was but one of a number that Hemingway realized "were excellent places for me to stay away from" [*AMF*, pp. 110]. Barney and Ezra Pound concocted a "Bel Esprit" scheme in which everyone would pitch in a percentage of his earnings to free T. S. Eliot from the bank so he could write poetry. If it worked for Eliot, everybody else would, in turn, be fixed up. Unfortunately, *The Waste Land*'s success landed Eliot "a lady of title," and the plan died. Hemingway claims he took the money he had earmarked for Eliot to the Enghein racetrack, where he struck it big betting "on jumping horses that raced under the influence of stimulants."

Barney's lesbianism was widely celebrated. Lynn theorizes that Hemingway made up Jacob "Jake" Barnes's name in part from her last name, Barney, and her street's name, Jacob. "Hemingway derived the name of a man who is passionately in love with a sexually aggressive woman with an androgynous first name [Brett] and a mannish haircut, a man whose dilemma is that, like a lesbian, he cannot penetrate his loved one's body with his own" [Lynn, p. 323].

12. Beach, Sylvia   18, Rue de l'Odéon
[apartment]   *[6th; Odéon]*

Sylvia Beach, proprietor of Shakespeare and Company, and her lover Adrienne Monnier lived here. Hemingway dined here often, escorted first by Hadley, then by Pauline.

In August 1944, Hemingway and his band of French *maquis* (Resistance fighters) liberated Beach and Monnier. Beach remem-

View of the Latin Quarter from the Hôtel Beauvoir.

bered he climbed to their apartment, machine gun in hand, "in battle dress, grimy and bloody" and took their last—next to last, Monnier claims—piece of soap to wash. In return, he and his men shot a Nazi sniper hiding on the rooftop. Then he rode off " 'to liberate . . . the cellar of the Ritz' " [Beach, pp. 219–20].

13. Hôtel Beauvoir   43, Avenue Georges Bernanos
[5th; Port Royal]
Hadley first stayed here with Bumby following Hemingway's decision in 1926 to leave her. Across the street from La Closerie, the six-story Beauvoir offers an impressive view of the Latin Quarter. From here, Hadley could have looked down on the sawmill apartment she had shared with Hemingway, the cafés they had dined in, and the Hôtel Venitia where he had slept with Pauline. A two-star hotel today, the Beauvoir has moderately priced rooms, the cheapest of which, however, do not offer a view of the Quarter.

14. Berkeley Hôtel

I, Rue de Ponthieu
[8th; F. D. Roosevelt]

Hemingway escorted "a beautiful girl . . . the mistress of some impressive industrialist or wine baron" to lunch at this famous hotel and restaurant in 1956. Mary Walsh Hemingway claimed she had herself proposed the girl to Hemingway "as a possible diversion." He returned after lunch and told Mary, "*On s'ennuyait à mourir*" (she bored me to death). Mary's response? "Poor lamb. Anyhow you're on a love-making diet. Or supposed to be" [Mary Hemingway, p. 442].

15. Black Sun Press

2, Rue Cardinale
[6th; St. Germain des Prés]

Located just off the quaint Place de Furstemberg that Henry Miller loved, the Black Sun Press printed limited editions of Hemingway's *Torrents of Spring* and *In Our Time*. It was run by Harry Crosby, nephew of John Pierpont Morgan, and his wife Caresse, who had patented the bra in 1914.

In 1928, Hemingway needed money to get himself and Pauline back to America. According to Caresse, she agreed to pay for the tickets in exchange for a new Hemingway piece on bullfighting. What she got was a thousand-word excerpt Hemingway had discarded from *A Farewell to Arms*. "I said that a five-page de luxe of Hemingway, signed at ten dollars a throw, would appear mighty precious to the public. An angry Hemingway demanded the manuscript back; 'No one can call Hemingway "precious" and get away with it'" [Caresse Crosby, p. 297].

Caresse wound up reprinting *In Our Time*, and Hemingway wound up with the tickets. Since he bought a Juan Gris painting about the same time, Crosby surmised "it was Gris and not the steamship line that cashed that check" [Caresse Crosby, p. 298].

The press is now gone, but the building that housed it remains.

16. Boeuf sur le Toit

28, Rue Boissy d'Anglas
[8th; Concorde]

Hemingway's 1923 *Star* readers learned that Jean Cocteau's Bull-on-the-Roof bar and dancing was "where everyone in Paris who believes that the true way to burn the candle is by igniting it at both ends goes," but not before 10:00 P.M. [*Dateline*, pp. 404–5]. So famous was the place that Kay Boyle claims people addressed mail to "Boeuf sur le Toit, The Universe." The name came from a Cocteau ballet, based on the story of a man who kept a menagerie of birds and a bull calf in his attic apartment. After a lengthy trial, the court ordered him to remove the animals. The former calf, now a full grown bull, was too big to expell, and so he remained *le boeuf sur le toit* [Boyle, pp. 320–21]. Where the Boeuf stood is today a store.

17. Bois de Boulogne   Porte Maillot

Count Mippipopoulous took Brett and Jake to dinner "at a restaurant in the Bois" [*SAR*, p. 61]. He could have picked from a number: Armenonville, Le Pré Catelan, Le Pavillon Royal, Le Pavillon Dauphine, Les Cascades, Le Clos Normand. In 1929, Julian Street in his *Where Paris Dines* called Armenonville and Le Pré Catelan "the two most attractive restaurants actually within the Bois," and raved over the "fairy lights" strung in the horse chestnut trees lining the lake fronting Armenonville's chalet. "Prices are not low," he adds. In *Across the River and Into the Trees*, Col. Richard Cantwell speaks of going to Armenonville. So let us leave Brett and Jake here.

Earlier, the Count had taken Brett to the Bois for a champagne breakfast. They probably polished off their "dozen bottles of Mumms" near Le Pré Catelan. Street's guide notes "it is an ancient custom of dissolute Parisians to breakfast here after wild nights in the city."

Both Armenonville and Le Pré Catelan remain well-known Bois restaurants.

18. Bookstalls

Seine
[5th; Place St. Michel]

Hemingway bought used books from the book stands that line the quais of the Seine. He favored those "*boîtes des bouqinistes*" that stood near tourist hotels such as the Tour d'Argent (15, Quai de la Tournelle; Hemingway says this famous restaurant rented rooms in his day) and the Hôtel du Quai Voltaire (19, Quai Voltaire). These sometimes had American books left behind by their clientele. His favorite *bouquiniste* judged books by their pictures and binding. "She had no confidence in books written in English" which were poorly bound and pictureless. "There is no way of judging them," she told the would-be author of the one true sentence [*AMF*, pp. 42–43].

Green metal and wood boxes whose fronts swing open into awnings, the Paris bookstalls resemble large footlockers bolted to the stone parapets of the Seine. Proprietors share the shade of their awnings with their inevitable chair, portable display shelf, and bric-a-brac. You can find comics wrapped in cellophane, engravings cut from books, postcards from around the world, French science fiction, defunct legal and medical texts, musty religious treatises, and hordes of dog-eared paperbacks.

Baedeker's says the *bouquinistes* originally shared the seventeenth-century Pont Neuf with con artists, jugglers, showmen, and junk dealers. Only the book dealers—now on the quais—remain.

151 bis, Boulevard du Montparnasse
19. Boulangerie *[6th; Vavin]*

Leaving his apartment over the sawmill on Rue Notre-Dame-des-Champs, Hemingway used to cut through this bakery's back door

Bookstalls lining the quais of the Seine with the Cathédrale Notre Dame in the background.

to gain the Boulevard. Entering by the back door, which opens onto an old stone staircase that spirals upwards, one would never expect to come out into a modern *boulangerie-patisserie* fronting on the busy Boulevard du Montparnasse but one does. *Quartier* residents still use the passage as a shortcut. As do Hemingway pilgrims who, in politeness, buy croissants in lieu of paying tariffs.

In the now-private basement off the staircase, Hadley found an upright piano she practiced on.

Place du Parvis Notre Dame
20. Cathédrale Notre Dame *[4th; Cité]*
Hemingway described for his *Star* readers two "hungry gargoyles, the one swallowing a long, luckless dog, while its companion gazes greedily down toward the land where France is now encamped" *[Dateline,* p. 369]. The land was Germany, and Hemingway took the two gargoyles on the northeast corner of the tower to represent French hatred of Germany. As he pointed out, "the cathedral is old, but these monstrosities are not"; they were erected by Viollet-le-Duc, whose twenty-year restoration of Notre Dame ended in 1864.

The still-hungry gargoyles can be seen if you take the tour of the Tours de Notre Dame. The view of Paris from the steeples alone is worth the admission price.

19, Rue d'Antin
21. Les Caves Murae *[2nd; Opéra]*
Hard though it may be to believe, this narrow café-bar is twice as wide as it was in Hemingway's day. The dining area was added by knocking out a wall. Now Aux Cloches de Villedieu, then Les Caves Murae, it was here Hemingway wrote Loeb that he could buy good whiskey at low prices. You can still buy good whiskey and beer in this restaurant-bar, which the genial proprietor says was also a favorite of Jacques Brel.

It was in Caves Murae that Hemingway announced to his friend Bill Bird that he was divorcing Hadley "because I am a son of a bitch" [Baker, *Ernest Hemingway,* p. 178]. Bird, who ran the continental offices of Consolidated Press, was a model for Jake Barnes, European director of the Continental Press Association. Both men got rid of unwelcome friends by taking them to a bar, sharing a drink, and leaving. Bird's favorite bar for this was Les

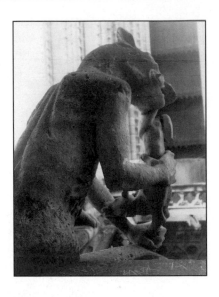

The Cathédrale Notre Dame, and a hungry gargoyle in the nearer tower.

Caves Murae. Jake gets rid of Cohn by going with him "down stairs to the café on the ground floor" [*SAR*, p. 11]. If Jake Barnes's fictional office exists in Paris, it is probably to be found over Aux Cloches de Villedieu.

22. Chappé, Claude   Boulevard St. Germain and Rue du Bac
[statue]   *[7th; Rue du Bac]*
Stood up at the Crillon by Brett, Jake leaves for the Rotonde. On the way, his taxi passes "the statue of the inventor of the semaphore engaged in doing same." No longer extant, the statue incorporated a telegraph pole behind Chappé (1763–1805), creating "un mauvais effet sculptural."

23. Chope de Nègre et   13, Rue du Faubourg Montmartre
Taverne des Sports   *[9th; Montmartre]*
In San Sebastian, Jake Barnes agrees to meet the bicycle team's manager at the Chope de Nègre where they will drink another *fine* (brandy) [*SAR*, pp. 236–37]. They may have drunk a *fine* there, but you won't; what was then the Chope de Nègre is today a tawdry fast-food café. And the "Rue du Faubourg Montmartre chic" that Barnes noted in the two French girls who followed the bikers is today on a par with the fast-food crowd.

What does remain is Paris. "There is only one Paname. In all the world, that is," Barnes and the manager had agreed. *Paname* was Devil's Island argot for Paris, since Panama was what you ran towards if you ran. Famous now as Edith Piaf's song, it was also the rallying cry of the Free French army in World War II. Hemingway told his red-haired companion Archie Pelkey on their way towards Paris in August 1944, " 'The French call it [Paris] *Paname* when they love it very much.'

" 'I see,' Archie said. '*Compris*. Just like something you might call a girl that wouldn't be her right name. Right?'

". . . 'Yeah,' I said. I couldn't say anything more then, because I had a funny choke in my throat and I had to clean my glasses because there now, below us, gray and always beautiful, was spread the city I love best in all the world" [*Collier's*].

                                                    Place Pasdeloup
24. Cirque d'Hiver   *[11th; Filles du Calvaire]*
In his preface to the book, Hemingway lists "the great twenty-round fights at the Cirque d'Hiver" as among those memories he

Cirque d'Hiver.

has left out of *A Moveable Feast*. He was forever dragging wives and friends to these boxing events, both here and at the now gone Cirque de Paris (18, Avenue de la Motte-Picquet).

Jake Barnes attended the LeDoux-Francis fight in Paris (location unknown) "the night of the 20th of June. It was a good fight" [*SAR*, p. 81]. The Charles (or Charlie) LeDoux–Kid Francis fight actually occurred on June 9, 1925; LeDoux—once bantamweight champ of Europe and featherweight champ of France—lost. He retired the next year. According to Hemingway, LeDoux was "one of the best infighters I have ever seen," but the war interrupted his career. Francis was a featherweight from Marseilles who had boxed as an Italian in the States.

3, Place du Tertre
25. Au Clairon des Chasseurs   *[18th; Abbesses]*
Hemingway and A. E. Hotchner stopped here in the fifties, at "the old restaurant where Ernest had sometimes eaten, when he had money to eat, during his early Paris days" [Hotchner, p. 42]. In the twenties, Montmartre still retained its village atmosphere; John Dos Passos is said to have wished his heart preserved in a pitcher of wine here [Morton, p. 258]. But today's Montmartre is a horrendous tourist trap crammed with everyone but Frenchmen. Cheek by jowl, they crowd the Place du Tertre, where sidewalk and con artists relieve them of whatever money the pickpockets haven't already found. And Au Clairon des Chasseurs, however quaint it may once have been, is hardly worth the trip.

Le Guide Michelin suggests visiting Place du Tertre early in the morning if you want to capture its *"air villageois."* When there are few tourists, Montmartre is worth a Métro ride.

171, Boulevard du Montparnasse
26. La Closerie des Lilas   *[6th; Port Royal]*
Hemingway's favorite café, La Closerie is around the corner from where Hemingway lived on Notre-Dame-des-Champs. Its tree-shaded terrace (horse chestnuts in Hemingway's day; plane trees in ours) looking out on Marshal Michel Ney's statue gives a taste of the country in Paris.

Here Hemingway and Dos Passos drank "some such innocuous fluid as vermouth cassis" and plotted Hemingway's new style based on "cablese and the King James Bible" [Dos Passos, pp. 141–42]. Here Hemingway wrote "The Big Two-Hearted River" and finished the first draft of *The Sun Also Rises*. In *A Moveable Feast* he remembers sitting here with his *cahiers*, pencils, and horse chestnut and rabbit's foot in his right pocket for luck.

He liked La Closerie because the Montparnasse crowd didn't. And he and Evan Shipman bemoaned its 1925 change of management that brought an American bar and clean-faced, white-coated waiters. The Milan family, which instituted these changes, still runs La Closerie. Today the bar seems traditional, the white

La Closerie des Lilas and its American bar, with Claude Thomas, bartender (bottom).

coats typically French. Nothing has changed since 1925, as an old photograph on the wall demonstrates. M. Milan claims bourbon was Hemingway's favorite drink, and you can drink it right where Hemingway drank his. On the bar is a small plaque to "E. Hemingway," marking his favorite spot; over the bar is a portrait of the artist as a young man.

28, Rue Vavin
27. College Inn *[6th; Vavin]*
Two bars located here in the twenties enjoyed Hemingway's patronage. Jimmie "the Barman" Charters says Hemingway came here when it was known as Pirelli's. As the College Inn, it was run by Jed Kiley. Hiler, who had painted the original Jockey's interior, painted this bar's also. Kiley's College Inn served "American food," Street wrote, and was "not precisely the place for the *jeune fille*" [Street, p. 233]. La Dolce Vita, a "cabaret spectacle," stands here today.

10, Place de la Concorde
28. Hôtel Crillon *[8th; Concorde]*
"When I had money, I went to the Crillon" to drink, Hemingway remembered in *A Moveable Feast [AMF*, p. 192]. You, too, had better have money to drink here; located in the Gabriel's palatial mansion on the Place de la Concorde, the Crillon—as a plaque in its lobby boasts—is one of the world's finest hotels. Stood up by Brett, Jake drinks "a Jack Rose with George the barman" in the Crillon bar.

113–117, Boulevard du Montparnasse
29. Damoy's *[6th; Vavin]*
Julien Damoy's, a chain *épicerie* with over two thousand branches in France, had a store here in 1925 that Jake Barnes and Bill Gorton pass by on their drunken stroll through Paris.

7, Rue Daunou
30. Daunou Club *[2nd, Opéra]*
Hemingway says he went to Daunou's, a defunct club located in the still extant Théâtre Daunou a few doors from Harry's New York Bar. The club featured dining and dancing. Woon notes "The Daunou Club—started simultaneously with the opening of the Théâtre Daunou by Jane Renouardt, who at first ran the club herself" [Woon, p. 236]. Both opened in 1921.

Aux Deux Magots.

31. Aux Deux Magots

170, Boulevard St. Germain
[6th; St. Germain des Prés]

Across the street from Lipp's, Aux Deux Magots—the *magots*, statues of Chinese monks, not maggots, are inside, left over from the hosiery store that once stood here—is celebrated in France as a favorite café of postwar existentialists such as Camus, Sartre, and Simone de Beauvoir.

Hemingway drank dry sherry here with James Joyce, "although

you will always read that he drank only Swiss white wine" [*AMF*, p. 128]. "We would go out to drink and Joyce would fall into a fight. He couldn't even see the man so he'd say: 'Deal with him, Hemingway! Deal with him!'" [Ellmann, p. 75].

Samuel Putnam remembered Hemingway at the Deux Magots. "The 'three most exciting things in life,' he gravely informed me, 'were flying, skiing, and sexual intercourse.' Only he did not say sexual intercourse but used the short and not unlovely word" [Putnam, p. 130].

The Deux Magots looks out across the square to St. Germain des Prés, the oldest church in Paris (eleventh century). Its umbrella-shaded terrace is still a hangout for artists and artistes, and for those willing to pay 16 francs for a coffee or 17 for a beer. You can sit among the famous and the would-be famous, or you can cross the square to the quieter and cheaper Café Bonaparte and watch people watch you watch them.

By 1927, Americans had—according to Reynolds—corrupted this French café, "Where one hears more dirty jokes and advice as to where to buy 'adorable dresses' all in English than anywhere else in Paris. The rampage of youths of Pep and Pocket book, and their Sub-Deb 'dates.' And also here, you find the sober-faced Frenchman and his wife, craning their ears to catch a word and stretching their eyes to study these strange specimens from America" [Reynolds, p. 205].

32. The Dingo Bar   10, Rue Delambre
                                         [14th; Vavin]

Around the corner from the Vavin crossroads, the Dingo is where an up-and-coming Hemingway first met literary king-of-the-mountain F. Scott Fitzgerald. They drank champagne, and before passing out Fitzgerald asked Hemingway, "Tell me, did you and your wife sleep together before you were married?" [*AMF*, p. 150].

"That girl with the phony title who was so rude and that silly drunk with her" were also there. These were Lady Duff Twysden and Pat Guthrie, models for *The Sun Also Rises'* Brett Ashley and Mike Campbell. Jimmie "the Barman" Charters recalled their doomed love affair in his memoirs *This Must Be the Place.* Guthrie dumped Twysden for an American girl just before their planned wedding; the girl introduced him to drugs. Bouncing one too many checks, he fled to South Africa, where a souring con scheme brought him back to Paris to die of an overdose of veronal.

Hemingway told Hotchner that Twysden married an American and moved to New Mexico where she died in 1938 of tuberculosis. "Her pallbearers had all been her lovers. . . . One of the grieving pallbearers slipped on the church steps and the casket dropped and split open" [Hotchner, p. 48]. Edward Morrill Cody, however, claimed Twysden was cremated and had no burial service.

The Dingo—French for "the mad one"—started as a nameless *bistro* whose French proprietor installed a bar, hired an English interpreter, and raked in expatriate dollars. After *The Sun Also Rises* appeared in 1926, tourist buses added the Vavin crossroads to their itinerary, and the Dingo advertised its literary connections.

The Dingo is now the restaurant Auberge du Centre. Its exterior and interior remain nearly unchanged since the twenties, and you can drink at the same bar Hemingway and Fitzgerald met at. Small and quiet, L'Auberge boasts a traditional and excellent

Auberge du Centre (The Dingo Bar), Monsieur and Madame Pierre Berthier, proprietors.

cuisine. Chef Pierre Berthier is friendly and willing to talk about the Hemingway connection.

33. Café du Dôme

108, Boulevard du Montparnasse
[14th; Vavin]

One of *the* expatriate hangouts in Paris, the Dôme was where Hemingway and Hadley headed after hitting France in December 1921. He wrote Sherwood Anderson, "Well here we are. And we sit outside the Dome Cafe . . . warmed up against one of those charcoal braziers and it's so damned cold outside and the brazier makes it so warm and we drink rum punch, and the rum punch enters us like the Holy Spirit" [*Selected Letters*, December, 1921]. It was Prohibition in America, Anderson was still Hemingway's mentor, and the rum punch didn't cost today's 35 francs.

Hemingway continued to prefer the Dôme to its nearby compatriots, the Rotonde and Select. In *A Moveable Feast*, he "passed the collection of inmates at the Rotonde and, scorning vice and the collective instinct," drank at the Dôme, because "there were people there who had worked" [*AMF*, p. 101]. But Sinclair Lewis,

The Dôme.

snubbed by the expatriate crowd as a "best seller," savaged the Dôme as "on a corner charmingly resembling Sixth avenue at Eighth street, and all the waiters understand Americanese, so that it is possible for the patrons to be highly expatriate without benefit of Berlitz. It is, in fact, the perfectly standardized place to which standardized rebels flee from the crushing standardization of America."

By 1934, a new kind of expatriate filled the Dôme. Hemingway told his *Esquire* readers that "The only foreigners you see are Germans. The Dome is crowded with refugees from the Nazi terror and Nazis spying on the refugees" [*Byline*, p. 155].

34. Enghien-les-Bains   Outside Paris

Hemingway and Hadley picnicked here in the summer and won 85 francs to 10 on the horses. They blew one good day's winnings on a meal at Prunier's afterwards. Hemingway told Hotchner that the old Enghien—replaced now by "unfriendly concrete"—was "my all-time-favorite track" [Hotchner, p. 39]. In *A Moveable Feast*, he paints a landscape of it: "It was early and we sat on my raincoat on the fresh cropped grass bank and had our lunch and drank from the wine bottle and looked at the old grandstand, the brown wooden betting booths, the green of the track, the darker green of the hurdles, and the brown shine of the water jumps and the whitewashed stone walls and white posts and rails, the paddock under the new leafed trees and the first horses being walked to the paddock" [*AMF*, p. 52].

35. L'Escargot
20 or 25, Rue de la Gaîté
[14th; Gaîté]

Hemingway, Pauline and the Crosbys dined at this *bistro* on oysters and white wine following a trip to the circus in 1927. Which address was L'Escargot's is unclear; across the street from each other, neither is today a restaurant. But it was probably number 20, today a porno movie house. The windmill on the facade, however, predates Hemingway, as does the building on the corner, which once housed "le terrible bal des Mille colonnes." These buildings were once part of the old Bobino Music Hall, which was called the Bal des Escargots in the nineteenth century.

The Rue de la Gaîté was once celebrated for "*ses bals, ses music-halls, ses crêpes, ses escargots, son beaujolais blanc*" [Fuss-Amoré and

Ombiaux]. There are two kinds of *escargots* in French cuisine, the larger *bourgognes* and the smaller *petits gris*. Hemingway reported that 70 percent of all snails sold in his day were actually beef. He suggested his *Star* readers "cross an inner tube with a live frog, and make the product slippery, and you have the texture" [*Dateline*, p. 374].

42, Rue du Montparnasse

36. Café Falstaff [14th; Vavin]

Jimmie "the Barman" Charters moved here after he left the Dingo. He took with him most of his clientele. According to Kay Boyle, who got the story from Hilaire Hiler, it was on the sidewalk here in 1929 that a 200-pound Hemingway beat up 115-pound Robert McAlmon.

A drunken Fitzgerald had told Hemingway that McAlmon was telling everyone that Hemingway was gay, Pauline a lesbian, and that Hemingway beat his wives, especially Hadley, whose son Bumby had been born prematurely after one such beating. Hemingway thought McAlmon, who was gay, "too pitiful to be beaten up," but felt he had to teach him a lesson [Baker, *Ernest Hemingway*, p. 206]. And did, beating him up on the sidewalk and then yelling at him, "Now tell that to your God-damn friends" [Bruccoli, p. 354].

The Falstaff is still open, its interior largely unchanged. You can see its white neon sign at night on the corner of the Boulevard du Montparnasse.

37. Fitzgerald, F. Scott and Zelda 14, Rue de Tilsitt
[apartment] [8th; Étoile]

The Fitzgeralds lived on the fifth floor of this fashionably located building from April 1925 until the end of the year. In *A Moveable Feast*, Hemingway remembered the apartment as "gloomy and airless," with no Fitzgerald belongings except "Scott's first books bound in light blue leather with the titles in gold." Fitzgerald showed Hemingway his ledgers, in which he had recorded over $113,000 he had earned since 1920. Much of it, Fitzgerald claimed, came from good stories he twisted to make "into saleable magazine stories." Hemingway called this "whoring," and told Fitzgerald to "Write the best story that you can write and write it as straight as you can" [*AMF*, p. 179].

F. Scott Fitzgerald and family in Paris, 1923. *(Princeton University Library, Sylvia Beach Collection)*

38. Fitzgerald, F. Scott and Zelda   10, Rue Pergolèse
[apartment]   *[16th; Argentine]*

Scott and Zelda Fitzgerald lived here from November 1929 until July 1930. He was working on *Tender is the Night* while Hemingway was revising *A Farewell to Arms*. Fitzgerald suggested to Hemingway a number of changes, which Hemingway resented, although he eventually incorporated them. Appended to a June 30 letter of Fitzgerald's suggestions is Hemingway's reaction, "Kiss my ass" [Fitzgerald, *Correspondence*, p. 228].

39. Flanner, Janet   36, Rue Bonaparte
[apartment]   *[6th; St. Germain des Prés]*

Hemingway used to visit Janet Flanner, Paris correspondent for *The New Yorker*, in her apartment in the Hôtel St. Germain des Prés. His chair, the only one large enough for Hemingway, had been designed for nursing mothers. They felt especially close, Flanner recalled, because both their fathers had committed suicide.

Formerly the Hôtel Napoleon Bonaparte, the Hôtel St. Germain des Prés is now a three-star hotel conveniently located near the heart of Hemingway's Paris. The desk clerk, who said guests occasionally ask for Flanner's room, had no idea which one it had been.

40. Fleischman, Leon
[apartment]   Near the Champs-Elysées

Leon Fleischman, retired from Boni and Liveright publishers, became their literary scout in Paris. Harold Loeb, who hoped his publisher Liveright might pick up Hemingway, took his mistress Kitty Cannell and Hemingway to Fleischman's apartment "near the Champs Elysées" one night [Loeb, pp. 226–27]. After an awkward evening, they left. Cannell reported that Hemingway called Fleischman and Loeb "double god damned kikes" upon leaving [Sarason, p. 147]. In *The Sun Also Rises*, Robert Cohn, based on Loeb, suffers a number of anti-Semitic slurs.

Fleischman's wife Helen divorced him and married James Joyce's son George.

                        172, Boulevard St. Germain
41. Café de Flore   *[6th; St. Germain des Prés]*

Another of Les Trois Grands, the Flore is so popular with foreigners that the Gault-Millau guidebook claims "you hardly hear a word of French spoken on the long terrace" during the summer [Gault-Millau, p. 182]. Hemingway alternated between the Flore and the Deux Magots, according to Mayfield, who remembered him writing in the café, "a young man upon whom assurance sat

Café de Flore.

like a horsehair plume upon the casque of a Garde Republicane" [Mayfield, pp. 135–36]. The simile is not that farfetched; Mayfield says the Garde did ride down the Boulevard.

Rue Blanche
42. Florence's   *[9th; Blanche]*

The true nightlife of Paris, Hemingway wrote his *Star* readers, did not get going until after three in the morning. And when it did get going, it went to Florence's. Florence, he wrote, was a black

American dancer, "jolly, funny, and wonderful on her feet." Her *pièce de résistance* was a number called "Everybody Steps." But it was an overly languid and English-accented Florence who said "So jolly to see you again" to Hemingway when he dropped by at 2:30 A.M. for poached eggs and buckwheat cakes. Discovered by the French nobility, Florence "ain't a Niggah no mo'," a waiter explained to him, adding she was now a Canadian Indian. Within the year, her entire staff was planning to cross over [*Dateline*, p. 406].

Street noted in his 1929 guide that Florence's was run by "a coloured woman who fancies snow-white evening gowns. Good American Negro jazz. A small place with tiny dance floor. Princeton, Yale, and Harvard will be there. Champagne compulsory" [Street, p. 247]. Reynolds's guide advised, "Go to Florence's if you don't go anywhere else" [Reynolds, p. 128].

43. Florida's   18, Rue de Clichy
[9th; Trinité]

Hemingway hung out at Florida's, a popular dance hall located next to the still extant Casino de Paris, his first year in Paris. It was especially popular with South Americans "with the biggest diamonds you ever gazed upon," given to singing their national anthems, according to Reynolds's guidebook. A chic after-midnight club for ballroom dancing to a jazz orchestra and tango band, Florida's charged "top price for champagne"—five dollars a quart [Reynolds, pp. 125–26].

44. Foyot's   22 bis, Rue de Vaugirard and 33, Rue de Tournon   *[6th; Odéon]*

Opened in 1848, closed in 1932, Foyot's earned *Baedeker's* approval as the best restaurant in the Latin Quarter. It was probably here that Ernest Walsh, tubercular editor of *This Quarter*, took Hemingway when they lunched at "a restaurant that was the best and the most expensive in the Boulevard St. Michel quarter." They washed down two dozen "expensive flat coppery *marennes*" with a bottle of Pouilly-fuissé, while Hemingway wondered if Walsh "ate the oysters in the same way the whores in Kansas City, who were marked for death and practically everything else, always wished to swallow semen as a sovereign remedy against the con" [*AMF*, pp. 124–25]. After the oysters, they polished off tournedos with sauce Bearnaise and a bottle of Chateauneuf du Pape. Walsh hinted Hemingway might receive the *Dial*'s $1,000 literary award—enough to live on and travel in Europe for nine months. But Hemingway did not get the money. Nor did Joyce, to whom Walsh had also hinted it might come.

Where Foyot's was is now a small park, across from the Palais du Luxembourg, the French Senate.

45. Gare de Lyon

Boulevard Diderot
[12th; Gare de Lyon]

Hadley took the train here for Lausanne to join Hemingway in December 1922. She brought with her all his manuscripts in a suitcase that she left on the train while she went to buy a bottle of Vittel water (Hemingway's version) or to chat with Hemingway's journalist friends (Hadley's version) on the quai. When she returned, the suitcase was gone.

When she told Hemingway, he rushed back to Paris to see if Hadley really had packed all the originals and carbons. She had. He lost all his early work except for "My Old Man" and "Up In Michigan," which were out at the time. Pound maintained Hadley, jealous of Hemingway's writing, deliberately lost the suitcase. Probably not, biographers think, though a number speculate that her losing his work meant she was fated to lose him.

46. Hôtel du Grand Cerf   Senlis, *outside Paris*

In *The Sun Also Rises* Jake suggests he and Cohn stay at the Grand Cerf after Cohn kicks him under the table for suggesting in front of Frances Clyne that they visit a girl in Strasbourg. And Loeb reveals he and Hemingway—without their wives—visited Senlis in October 1924. A hotel-room poker game almost ruined their friendship. At first Loeb cleaned out Hemingway, who insisted on writing IOUs he couldn't meet. Then Hemingway took pleasure in seeing Loeb lose his shirt to him. Loeb had learned, he tells us, that Hemingway "disliked defeat" [Loeb, pp. 216–17].

Thirty-three miles from Paris, the Grand Cerf, famous for its food, cost 35 francs a night in those days.

Hemingway probably passed through Senlis again during World War II on what Baker calls "the most foolhardy of his wartime adventures." Egged on by a note taunting him that the Ritz wasn't where the action was, Hemingway drove out of Paris

in a jeep through German-occupied territory to prove himself
[Baker, *Ernest Hemingway*, pp. 420–21].

47. Hôtel du Grand Veneur   Rambouillet, *outside Paris*
Thirty miles outside Paris, this still well-known hotel became
Hemingway's headquarters during the Allied rush towards Paris
in 1944. Two days ahead of the American army, he and two
other Americans had more Germans surrendering than they could
handle. Hemingway's solution, according to Collins and Lapierre,
was to take the Germans' pants off and put the men to peeling
potatoes in the hotel kitchen for the French forces.

48. Guaranty Trust Company of   I, Boulevard des Italiens
New York   *[2nd; Opéra]*
Hemingway's bank and mail drop during his early years in Paris,
probably because Hadley's cousin Bates Wyman worked here.
Alice Sokoloff in her biography of Hadley claims Wyman was a
snob who looked down on Hemingway as an "artistic bum." In
revenge, the Hemingways would take him slumming to the Bal
du Printemps [Sokoloff, pp. 55–56].

A rich American expatriate and painter, Gerald Murphy de-
posited $400—over 13,000 francs, half a year's income—in Hem-
ingway's account when he was broke in 1926. He also lent him his
studio apartment when Hemingway dumped Hadley. In return,
Hemingway put him in the end of *A Moveable Feast* as one of "the
rich [who] came led by the pilot fish." In a portion he deleted,
Hemingway says the Murphys "only backed me in every ruthless
and evil decision that I made" [Baker, *Ernest Hemingway*, p. 593].

5, Rue Daunou
49. Harry's New York Bar   *[2nd; Opéra]*
Opened in 1923 by Harry McElhone, a Scot bartender, Harry's
soon achieved celebrity status among Americans. McElhone re-
created in Paris "something to bring tears to the eyes of a sen-
timentalist during Prohibition," Al Laney of the *Paris Herald* explains—saloon doors, bar mirror, back room, an American bar, a
free lunch. And an "International Barflies" club open to one and
all [Laney, pp. 187–88].

And the place hasn't changed since. College pennants crowd

all walls except for the one papered with money. The doors still swing—and warn you to look out for them. McElhone's address is painted outside in phonetic French for American tourists: "SANK ROO DOE NOO."

Hotchner says Hemingway grew tired of the false collegiate scene. "'All they need,' Ernest said, under his breath, 'is Noel Coward leading a community sing'" [Hotchner, p.45]. But Hemingway credits Harry's with helping his career. After having thrown out a lion that shit on the floor and its irate ex-pug owner, Hemingway figured he'd better "put my juice into a book instead" [Hotchner, pp. 45–46]. The book was *A Farewell to Arms*.

50. Hemingway, Ernest   38, Rue Descartes
[studio]   *[5th; Monge]*

The Rue Mouffetard turns into Rue Descartes as you leave Place de la Contrescarpe and head towards the Seine. In a narrow section of small restaurants is number 39, where French poet Paul Verlaine died and where Hemingway rented an eighth-floor room for 60 francs a month. Here he composed his first European sketches, using the Corona typewriter (he called it "this mitrailleuse"—machine gun) Hadley had bought him. In *A Moveable Feast*, he remembers the fireplace into which he threw chestnut hulls and mandarin orange peels, and the bottle of kirsch he kept for warming himself at the end of the day.

51. Hemingway, Ernest   69, Rue Froidevaux
[apartment]   *[14th; Gaîté]*

Hemingway borrowed this studio apartment from Gerald Murphy in August 1926 after he separated from Hadley. Across the street from Montparnasse Cemetery, it stood between a *pompes funèbres* —funeral home—and a tombstone store. The studio's thirty-foot-high walls were hung with Murphy's modernist paintings. Holed up here, Hemingway finished correcting proofs of *The Sun Also Rises*. When he mailed them to Scribner's on August 27, he had added a dedication, "THIS BOOK IS FOR HADLEY AND JOHN HADLEY NICANOR." Later, he wrote Hadley, explaining she had rights to the royalties to the novel:

> It is the only thing that I who have done so many things to hurt you can do to help you—and you must let me do it. . . .
> You supported me while they were being written and helped

me write them. I would never have written any of them In
Our Time, Torrents or The Sun if I had not married you and
had your loyal and self-sacrificing and always stimulating
and loving—and actual cash support backing. . . . [you] who
are the best and truest and loveliest person that I have ever
known. [Meyer, pp. 181–82]

52. Hemingway, Ernest and   74, Rue du Cardinal Lemoine
Hadley *[apartment]*   *[5th; Monge]*

The Hemingways lived on the third floor here during their first
stay in Paris. Located over a noisy *bal musette* and an herbalist's,

Hemingway's first apartment in Paris was on the third
floor of this building; an herbalist and her grand-
daughter stand in the doorway of her shop, which
is still open for business on the first floor.

the place was cheap. Across the street was a *boucherie chevaline* and a wine co-op. There is still a dance club on the first floor, and Simone, the red-haired herbalist, today tells of sitting with Hemingway on her doorstoop and trading stories: *"Il a bouvait beaucoup. Il m'a dit, 'attention, Simone, je te mettrais dans un livre.'"* ("He drank a lot. He told me, 'Take care, Simone, I'll put you in a book.'")

In *A Moveable Feast*, Hemingway remembers a cold water, two-room flat with only a slop jar for a toilet, and "a fine view and a good mattress . . . and pictures we liked on the wall" [*AMF*, p. 37]. The scaling facade of number 74 leans back from the street as do so many old Parisian buildings. Its first floor is pierced by a hallway that leads to the tightly spiraled stairs. There are three apartments on each floor. The slopwagons Hemingway heard at night are gone, the "squat toilets" he remembered on each landing are now connected to the city sewer by white pipes that snake down the backside of the building.

[NOTE: Gertrude Stein claims the Hemingways' first apartment was off the Place du Tertre; the *Guide littérarie de la France* claims Hemingway lived on the Place des Vosges; and Root claims he stayed in a *pension de famille* on the corner of Rues Soufflot and St. Jacques. I can verify none of these.]

53. Hemingway, Ernest and   113, Rue Notre-Dame-des-Champs
Hadley *[apartment]*   *[6th; Port Royal]*

An unremarkable modern building stands where the Hemingways once "trouved an appt . . . semi furnished over a saw mill on a 3 mos to 3 mos to 3 mos etc. basis," as Hemingway wrote Pound in February 1924 [*Letters*, p. 110]. The noisy sawmill explained the cheap rent. But the sawmill bothered Hemingway; he mentions "the sudden whine of the saw" in *Green Hills of Africa* [*GHA*, p. 70], and says in *A Moveable Feast* an unwelcome conversation was "soothing as the noise of a plank being violated in the sawmill." The landlady, Madame Chautard, was a "mad woman" whose pet dog Hemingway would immortalize in *The Sun Also Rises*.

Fitzgerald visited here, one time arriving so drunk that he sat in the fireplace. William Carlos Williams stopped by to circumcise Bumby, noting "He naturally cried, to his parents' chagrin." And

Archibald MacLeish remembered the apartment in his poem, "The Human Season":

The lad in the Rue de Notre Dame des Champs
At the carpenter's loft on the left-hand side going down—
The lad with a supple look like a sleepy panther—
And what became of him? Fame became of him.
Veteran out of the wars before he was twenty:
Famous at twenty-five; thirty a master—
Whittled a style for his time from a walnut stick
In a carpenter's loft in a street of that April city.

All that remains from that April city apartment is the stone-flagged courtyard, which can be reached by entering number 117.

54. Hemingway, Ernest and   6, Rue Férou
Pauline *[apartment]*   *[6th; St. Sulpice]*
Hemingway moved in here with his second wife, Pauline Pfeiffer, whom he had married in May 1927. Pfeiffer, a writer for the Paris *Vogue*, is P.O.M.—Poor Old Mama—in *Green Hills of Africa*. But by *A Moveable Feast* she has become "rich . . . using the oldest trick

Hemingway and Pauline, around 1927. *(Courtesy Ernest Hemingway Collection, John F. Kennedy Library)*

there is. It is that an unmarried young woman becomes the temporary best friend of another young woman who is married, goes to live with the husband and wife and then unknowingly, innocently and unrelentingly sets out to marry the husband" [*AMF*, pp. 209–11]. Which, according to all accounts, is exactly what Pfeiffer did —while Hemingway's friends watched.

Pfeiffer's rich uncle Gus paid for the seven-room apartment located on the quiet street a block from the Luxembourg Gardens. Hemingway's second wife was not the sort to live over a sawmill and use a common toilet. Her marriage lasted until 1940, when Hemingway left her for Martha Gelhorn.

It was in this apartment that Hemingway wrote *A Farewell to Arms*.

55. Hemingway, Hadley   35, Rue de Fleurus
[apartment]   *[6th; St. Placide]*

Hadley and Bumby took a sixth-floor apartment here following the collapse in 1926 of her marriage to Hemingway. He moved her in, using a wheelbarrow to cart her belongings over. These included Joan Miró's "The Farm," which he had given her and would later "borrow" indefinitely. Baker says he burst into tears after dropping off the first load.

An imperfect husband, Hemingway was a better father, taking Bumby for strolls in the Luxembourg Gardens and for ice creams in the cafés while Hadley thought things out. One day, harmonica in hand and mouth ringed with vanilla ice cream, Bumby looked up at Hemingway and exclaimed, "*la vie est beau avec papa*" [Baker, *Ernest Hemingway*, pp. 177–78]. And Hemingway, taken with Bumby's cries of "Papa! Papa!" that summer, urged everyone to call him "Papa." And so the nickname was born.

The building Hadley lived in was demolished the summer of 1988.

56. Henri Quatre   Square du Vert Galant, Île de la Cité
[statue]   *[1st; Pont Neuf]*

A favorite fishing spot for Parisians, this spot of chestnut-shaded green stands on the prow of the Île de la Cité. Hemingway remembers it in *A Moveable Feast*. The original statue, erected in 1635, was melted down during the Revolution. Louis XVII had it replaced in 1818 with the current statue, made of metal from

Statue of Henri Quartre on the Île de la Cité.

Napoleon's statue which once stood on the Vendôme Column. Legend has it that the smelter, a Bonapartist, hid a statue of Napoleon and Bonapartist tracts in the statue's right arm. Henri Quatre (1589–1610) was a *vert galant*—ladies' man—hence the name of the square.

57. Hippodrome d'Auteuil
Bois de Boulogne
[Port d'Auteuil]

Hemingway reminisced in *A Moveable Feast* about his and Hadley's trips here. Though he never made money betting the horses, he justified it because he wrote about them. All these early stories are lost, however, except for "My Old Man," an Anderson-like story that includes a description of the 4,500-meter steeplechase at Auteuil. *Best Short Stories* of 1923 included "My Old Man," and the volume was dedicated to "Hemenway"; the editor misspelled the unknown author's name.

Hotchner, Hemingway, and Mary Hemingway attended the races here in the 1950s. Hemingway thought the stands a scene worthy of Degas. " 'It would be truer on his canvas than what we now see. That is what the artist must do . . . capture the thing so truly that its magnification will endure. That is the difference between journalism and literature.'" Then he looked at his racing form; " 'This is the true art of fiction,' he said" [Hotchner, pp. 39–40].

58. The Hole in the Wall Bar

23, Boulevard des Capucines
[2nd; Opéra]

Le Trou dans le Mur is a narrow bar with a red-painted facade that looks today much as it must have in Hemingway's day. It was here

The Hole in the Wall Bar.

Hemingway supposes that Pound bought the opium he gave him in *A Moveable Feast*. A hangout for deserters during World War I, the bar supposedly had an exit into the sewers of Paris. Rumors of such bolt holes abound in the area; the Phantom of the Paris Opera, who hovered nearby, had one. These days drugs have also moved underground; deals are made at several well-known Métro stops. Drugs were cheaper in the twenties: "In such places hashish . . . went for about a dollar a joint—New York prices— to tourists, and five to the dollar to . . . wised-up consumers—" [Wolff, p. 162].

Hotchner claims that it was at Le Trou dans le Mur—not Lipp's, as Baker claims—that Hemingway waited three nights in a row for an angry Harold Loeb—whom Hemingway had savaged as Robert Cohn in *The Sun Also Rises*—to shoot him [Hotchner, pp. 47–48]. Loeb wasn't the only expatriate angered by Hemingway's novel; Jimmy "the Barman" Charters claims the joke in Montparnasse circles that year was that there were six characters in search of an author—with a gun.

59. Le Jardin du Luxembourg

Place Edmond Rostand
[6th; Luxembourg]

Once the haunt of Marie de Medicis, the Luxembourg was one of hungry Hemingway's favorite places. He went to the Musée

Le Jardin du Luxembourg.

du Luxembourg instead of eating lunch. "Belly-empty, hollow-hungry," he learned from Cezanne how to write, he says in *A Moveable Feast* [*AMF*, p. 69]. The museum also served for love; he met Pauline here when Hadley was away. The paintings Hemingway studied are now in the Musée d'Orsay.

Legend has it that a starving Hemingway killed pigeons at the Medici fountain, smuggling them out of the park under Bumby's baby blanket. Hotchner may have been the first to report it, but *Islands in the Stream* made it famous. In that book, Thomas Hudson remembers killing the pigeons with a slingshot and taking them "to the flat where we lived over the sawmill" [*IS*, p. 60].

60. Le Jardin des Plants   40, Rue Geoffroy Saint Hilaire
[5th; Monge]

Hemingway wrote his father that he used this zoo to identify French birds he was unfamiliar with. He also watched people watching animals, writing once about two Senegalese soldiers who teased the king cobra in the snake house.

His *Star* readers learned a lesson in Parisian boorishness thanks to Le Jardin. Confronted by a locked reptile house whose sign said it was open, Hemingway queried the guard. " 'What business is that of yours?' said the guard, and slammed the door" [*Dateline*, p. 137].

The garden may also be entered from its Seine side, across from the Gare d'Austerlitz.

61. Le Jardin des Tuileries   Place de la Concorde
[1st; Concorde]

Hemingway reserved the Tuileries for lovers. In *A Moveable Feast*, he and Hadley stop here at night on their way home from Prunier's and look through the Arc du Carrousel at the lights of the Concorde and beyond towards the Arc de Triomphe. Jake Barnes and Geogette Hobin pass through the Tuileries as well. He removes her hand from his crotch, telling her he's sick.

Georgette supposes Jake's sickness the French disease. Or the English disease; it depends which side of the Channel you're on. But he is hurt far worse than she supposes. Hotchner found out what we all wonder—just what was Jake missing. He asked Hemingway, " 'But Jake didn't have his balls shot off, did he?'

" 'No. . . . His testicles were intact. That was all he had, but this made him capable of feeling everything that a normal man feels but not able to do anything about it' " [Hotchner, pp. 47–48].

62. Le Jockey Club

127, Boulevard du Montparnasse
[6th; Vavin]

Hemingway called it "the best night club that ever was" [Hotchner, p. 52], and its fame is legendary. Decorated by Hilaire Hiler, painted by Utrillo, the Jockey drew the likes of Kiki, who sang barracks songs to the accompaniment of a piano-playing cowboy, and Josephine Baker, who danced the night away clad only in a black fur coat—if you believe Hemingway, who claims he stole her from a British soldier.

Baker took Paris by storm in 1925. Janet Flanner later recalled Baker's first appearance in La Revue Nègre at the Théâtre des Champs-Elysées: "She made her entry entirely nude except for a pink flamingo feather between her limbs; she was being carried upside down and doing the split on the shoulder of a black giant. Midstage he paused, and with his long fingers holding her basketwise around her waist, swung her in a slow cartwheel to the stage floor, where she stood, like his magnificent discarded burden, in an instant of complete silence. She was an unforgettable female ebony statue" [*Paris Was Yesterday*, p. xx].

A scandalized, mesmerized Paris fell in love with her. "JOSEPHINE! CACHE TON BOTTOM" screamed one headline [Laney, p. 181]. She performed at the Folies-Bergère and opened her own nightclub—Chez Josephine Baker—in Montmartre. After over fifty years of dancing, she died in 1975. The French honored her with a twenty-one-gun salute, the Légione d'honneur, and the Medaille de la Résistance.

Today's Jockey is across and down the street from where its predecessor stood at 146 Boulevard du Montparnasse on the corner of the Rue Campagne Première. With an enviable seafood spread and a pleasing decor, the Jockey seems a great place. But gourmet guides Gault and Millau mourn the passing of its early splendour: "*Les glorieux Jockey, où défile le monde entier de Hemingway à Blaise Cendrars, offre aux touristes hollandais et aux commerçants du Dusseldorf des spectacles désespérants qui ont pourtant l'air de les enchantes.*" (The glorious Jockey, where passed the entire world from Hemingway to Blaise Cendrars, offers Dutch tourists and Dussledorf businessmen sad shows which, however, seem to please them.)

63. Joyce, James   9, Rue de l'Université
[apartment]   *[7th; Rue du Bac]*

James Joyce was living here when Hemingway first moved to Paris, bearing with him a letter of introduction:

> Dear Mr. Joyce—I am writing you this note to make you acquainted with my friend Ernest Hemingway, who with Mrs. Hemingway is going to Paris to live, and will ask him to drop it in the mails when he arrives there.
>
> Mr. Hemingway is an American writer instinctively in touch with everything worth while going on here and I know you will find both Mr. and Mrs. Hemingway delightful people to know.
>
> They will be at 74 Rue du Cardinal Lemoine.
>
> Sincerely,
>
> Sherwood Anderson
>
> [Joyce, *Letters*, vol. III, pp. 54–55]

Anderson had written Hemingway identical letters of introduction to all the literary luminaries of the expatriate circle. Hemingway was much taken with Joyce; he wrote Anderson in 1922 that *Ulysses* was "a most goddamn wonderful book," and helped Sylvia Beach smuggle copies of the banned novel into America. Hemingway's copy of the first edition has many uncut pages; he read the beginning and end, but skipped the middle.

64. Joyce, James   2, Square de Robiac, 192, Rue de Grenelle
[apartment]   *[7th; La Tour Maubourg]*

Hemingway attended a reading of *Anna Livia Plurabelle* in Joyce's apartment here the first week of November 1927. Joyce had invited some twenty-five people to the reading, including Sylvia Beach, Robert McAlmon, and William Bird. McAlmon remembers the group as being dreadfully serious about the whole thing. He says Hemingway praised the passage as "actually giv[ing] one the feeling of night and of the flowing river." But McAlmon adds he once knew a Polish actress so good she could make an audience weep when she recited the alphabet [McAlmon, pp. 312–14].

In *Green Hills of Africa*, Hemingway remembers having Joyce and his wife Nora over to supper the night before he and Pauline left for Africa. Hemingway and Joyce got drunk, and Joyce kept quoting a phrase that was to run through *Finnegans Wake*: "*fraîche et rose, comme au jour de la bataille*" [*GHA*, p. 51]. It's a misquote of Edgar Quinet's comment on flowers, "*fraîches et riantes comme aux jours des batailles*," but it stuck with Hemingway. Mary Hemingway says he used it in Paris in 1944 when speaking "of a girl, a book, a wine, an aphorism" [Mary Hemingway, p. 134].

65. Kiley's

6, Rue Fontaine
[9th; Blanche]

Hemingway and Lady Duff Twysden popped up in John Gerald "Jed" Kiley's club one night soon after *The Sun Also Rises* appeared. Kiley liked Hemingway but had, according to his memoir, little use for him as a writer. He says Twysden was the only woman permanently barred from his nightclub, but he let her in then because of Hemingway, who surprised Kiley because he "Had a *smoking* (jacket) on and was even shaved" [Kiley, pp. 33–34].

McAlmon claims Hemingway's infatuation with Twysden pre-dated the novel's publication and Hemingway's separation from Hadley. He remembers Hemingway "actually paying drink bills for her and Pat Guthrie" in Montmartre. Hemingway even asked McAlmon "to take the weeping Hadley, then his wife, home while he stayed back with Brett" [Sarason, p. 227].

Kiley's enjoyed a short-lived popularity, even making it into the guidebooks of the twenties. The Prince of Wales himself patronized it, and is said to have served drinks during a waiters' strike. Kiley managed a series of nightclubs, including one at 25, Rue Fontaine. He is said to have blown his fortune cornering the ice cream market one summer, only to discover that the French would not eat ice cream in the winter.

66. Larbaud, Valery
[apartment]

71, Rue du Cardinal Lemoine
[5th; Monge]

Down the street from Hemingway's first apartment, Larbaud's rooms were where Joyce lived several months before the Hemingways arrived in Paris. Hemingway met the French writer Larbaud through Sylvia Beach, and they became friends.

68–70, Boulevard du Montparnasse
67. Lavenue's *[5th; Montparnasse Bienvenue]*

Hemingway, Loeb, and Cannell dined here as do their fictional counterparts Barnes, Cohn, and Clyne in *The Sun Also Rises*. The fictional meal opens the novel; the actual meal marked Loeb's departure from Paris. Loeb remembered, "The waiter gave Lily [Kitty Cannell], whom he knew well, the breast of roast duck; Hem got a helping of the lower anatomy. He glowered" [Loeb, p. 300].

On the way home, Hemingway told Cannell about *The Sun Also Rises*. "I'm writing a book with a plot and everything. Everybody's in it. And I'm going to tear those two bastards apart [Loeb and Bill Smith]. But not you, Kitty. I've always said you were a wonderful girl! I'm not going to put you in it" [Sarason, p. 149]. But, of course, he did put her in it—as Frances Clyne.

Though both Loeb and Hemingway write about "L'Avenue's," the correct spelling is Lavenue's—as is plainly indicated on the carved stone building that held M. Lavenue's hotel and restaurant. They were both among the best on the Left Bank, highly recommended in numerous guidebooks. Some French bemoaned Montparnasse's increasing popularity with foreigners; Bayard complains that

> *Aujourd'hui, que des disparitions ou d'embourgeoisement! A côté du Lavenue, devenue un établissement 'chic' (au sens cossu du mot) plutot qu'intellectuel, on ne voit guére que rivalité dans le confort, et les artistes étrangers ont fait des cafés de la Rotonde (particuliérment) et du Dôme des foyers surtout cosmopolites.* (Today, nothing but closings or turning bourgeois! At Lavenue's, now 'chic' [as in costly] rather than intellectual, you'll see nothing but friendly rivalry, and foreign artists have turned the Rotonde [especially] and the Dôme cafés into cosmopolitan clubs.) [Bayard, p. 157]

157–159, Boulevard du Montparnasse
68. Lavigne's *[6; Vavin]*

A five-minute walk from the sawmill apartment, M. Lavigne's Le Nègre de Toulouse Restaurant saw the Hemingways regularly enough to award them their own "red and white checkered napkins" [*AMF*, p. 99]. Lavigne served Hemingway's favorite wine, Cahors, in carafes, which Hemingway diluted with water.

He first ate with Loeb here, after meeting him at Ford's *transatlantic review* office. Ford, too, dined here with Hemingway, who put him in *The Sun Also Rises* as the Braddocks. Jake Barnes introduces the French prostitute Georgette Hobin to the Braddocks' dinner party here, and Georgette says of Lavigne's, "It isn't chic, but the food is all right."

Le Nègre de Toulouse is now La Pizzaria, its glassed-in terrace jutting out onto the Boulevard sidewalk. A pizzaria isn't exactly Hemingway's Paris, however; older Frenchmen recall that pizzas did not become popular until after the Second World War. Nor are French pizzas like American; they come one to a customer topped with oddities such as artichokes and fried eggs. In lieu of red peppers, the French douse them with spiced oil. The best, generally scorched, are cooked in ovens fired with wood.

69. Lerda Gymnasium

26, Rue de Pontoise
[5th; Maubert Mutualité]

Hemingway sparred at M. Lerda's Boxing Club du Quartier Latin during his early years in Paris. He made 10 francs a round as a partner with French professional heavyweights. The gym, located at the end of a courtyard, now provides lessons in judo, karate, jogging and yoga, but not boxing.

Hemingway loved boxing, taking in fights whenever he could, and tried to teach other expatriates such as Pound its finer points.

70. Lipp's

151, Boulevard St. Germain
[6th; St. Germain des Prés]

A hungry Hemingway treated himself to *cervelas remoulade, pommes à l'huile*, and a *distingué* (liter) of Kronenbourg beer here after Sylvia Beach handed him 600 francs he got from the German magazine *Der Querschitt* (*The Cross Section*) for which he had written "some rather obscene poems and published a long story."

One of Les Trois Grands, Lipp's was popular with the literati, according to Robert's 1925 guidebook, and filled with editors, actors, booksellers and students. Gault-Millau praise it as their "*brasserie préférée*." You can still get the *cervelas*, a house specialty, and the *distingué*, now called *serieux*. The *cervelas remoulade*, a sort

Lipp's.

of hot dog covered in mayonnaise, cost 33 francs in 1988; the copious *serieux* was cheaper and more filling.

Angered by their portraits in *The Sun Also Rises*, a number of expatriates swore they would kill Hemingway. Letting these "six characters in search of the author—with a gun" know he would be at Lipp's weekends, unarmed, Hemingway waited. "No bullets whistled," he wrote Fitzgerald.

In August 1944 Hemingway liberated Lipp's. Its jubilant *patron* produced a bottle of Fine Martel Trois Étoiles cognac, which a thirsty Hemingway polished off before glasses could be found.

71. Loeb, Harold   16, Rue de Monttessuy
[apartment]   *[7th; Alma Marceau]*

Harold Loeb and his mistress Kitty Cannell—models for *The Sun Also Rises'* Robert Cohn and Frances Clyne—lived in adjacent apartments here in the shadow of the Eiffel Tower. Loeb threw a party in the spring of 1925 to celebrate publication of his book *Doodab* and Hemingway's *In Our Time*. The two couples were joined by two Arkansas sisters, Pauline and Virginia Pfeiffer. Pauline, ostensibly in Paris with *Vogue*, was really looking for a husband, Cannell surmised. Rich and chic, Pauline viewed a shabbily dressed Hadley with sympathy (Hemingway had taken Stein's advice to put his money into things other than clothes). At the same time, Hemingway's fine form met with her approval.

Pauline became Hemingway's lover within the year and his wife within two. And Loeb dumped Cannell, whose loss to Lady Duff Twysden is chronicled in Loeb's *The Way It Was* and Hemingway's *The Sun Also Rises*.

72. MacLeish, Archibald   23, Rue Las Cases
[apartment]   *[7th; Solferino]*

American poet Archibald MacLeish lived here in the shadow of l'Église Ste. Clothilde in 1924. That summer, he met Hemingway for the first time at La Closerie des Lilas. They became good friends, often dining together.

73. MacLeish, Archibald   41, Avenue Foch
[apartment]   *[16th; Victor Hugo]*

The MacLeishes stayed rent-free in 1926 in this twelve-room apartment that Pierpont Morgan Hamilton (J. P. Morgan's nephew) lent them. They had to pay the nine-member staff's salaries, which nearly broke them. Years later, MacLeish remembered the butler's dismay when he and Hemingway came "in from the Bois and smelling" after biking [*Letters*, p. 36].

Formerly the Avenue du Bois de Boulogne, the street was renamed in 1930.

74. MacLeish, Archibald   44, Rue du Bac
[apartment]   *[7th; Rue du Bac]*
Hemingway stole a corkscrew from MacLeish the first time he
dined here. MacLeish had bought the apartment in 1927. Good
friends and bicycle enthusiasts, they watched the six-day races at
the Vélodrome d'Hiver together and biked constantly, riding as
far as Chartres. In World War II, Hemingway credited these bike
trips with giving him his knowledge of the terrain.

                                              Place de la Madeleine
75. La Madeleine   *[8th; Madeleine]*
Passing through Paris in 1918 on his way to the Italian Front,
a nineteen-year-old Hemingway saw a shell from a Big Bertha
explode at the rear of this church. He had been chasing the gun's
targets all afternoon in hopes of getting a story for the *Kansas City
Star*, which he had just quit. Four years later, he showed Hadley
where St. Luke's statue had lost its head in the explosion. Unlucky
Luke, still headless, has inscribed beneath him, *"Le 30 mai 1918
jour de la fête dieu un obus allemand a frappé l'église de la Madeleine
et decapité cette statue."* (On Corpus Christi day, May 30, 1918, a
German shell struck the Church of the Madeleine and decapitated
this statue.)

                                                    3, Rue Royale
76. Maxim's   *[8th; Concorde]*
World-famous Maxim's did not impress a young Hemingway,
who told *Star* readers trapped in Toronto that the restaurant was
"dull." "Full of profiteers, American buyers, and the inevitable
sprinkling of South Americans," Maxim's was a noisy, overlit,
barnlike place good only for "a headache" [*Dateline*, p. 407].

                                              29, Rue des Saints Pères
77. Michaud's   *[6th; St. Germain des Prés]*
The once-celebrated restaurant Michaud's had been a brasserie
for nearly ten years when its bathroom entered literary history
thanks to *A Moveable Feast*'s "A Matter of Measurements." Here
Hemingway reassured Scott Fitzgerald that the latter's natural endowments were as grand as his literary ones. According to Hemingway, Zelda had complained that Scott could not satisfy her: "it
was a matter of measurements." Adjourning to "le office," Hem-

La Madeleine (front of church), with the headless statue of St. Luke (top).

ingway regarded Fitzgerald. "There's nothing wrong with you. You look at yourself from above and you look foreshortened. Go over to the Louvre and look at the people in the statues and then go home and look at yourself in the mirror in profile."

Today Michaud's is the brasserie L'Escorailles. It is difficult to imagine Hemingway regarding a half-naked Fitzgerald in the pink-tiled unisex toilet whose door does not lock. Typical of many French toilets, its urinal is disconcertingly public. The more private toilet is a WC *turc* (Turkish toilet), like those Hemingway remembered from his first apartment: "squat toilets . . . with the two cleated cement shoe-shaped elevations on each side of the aperture so a *locataire* would not slip" [*AMF*, p. 3]. (To be fair, the bathroom was remodeled in the fifties.)

No one at L'Escorailles has heard of Hemingway or Fitzgerald. But they know Michaud's was "*trés célèbre*." For a poor Hemingway and Hadley, Michaud's was "exciting and expensive"; they ate here when flush from the races. James Joyce, however, ate here regularly with his family.

78. Ministère des Affaires Étrangers
37, Quai d'Orsay
[7th; Invalides]

As a reporter, Hemingway came to know the French Foreign Office located here. Jake Barnes covered the same press conferences, finding them as useless as had Hemingway. Riding back to his office near the Opéra, Jake pays two francs for a taxi; today, you pay twice that for a Métro ticket.

79. Moulin Rouge
Place Blanche
[18th; Blanche]

On most tourists' must lists, the Moulin Rouge remains synonymous with the cancan and the Gay Nineties. In Hemingway's day, the best seat from which to view "100 girls who do not wear even a bangle" cost $2.00, Reynolds's guide revealed [Reynolds, p. 134]. For his *Star* readers, Hemingway described the Moulin, crowded with shop girls and their men spotlit by revolving colored lights, as "one of the few places where the foreigners come into contact with French people taking their pleasure" [*Dateline*, p. 406].

80. Café-glacier Napolitain

51, Boulevard des Capucines
[2nd; Opéra]

A hangout for journalists, the Napolitain is where Jake and Cohn go for an *apéritif* in *The Sun Also Rises*. Afterwards, Jake watches "it get dark and the electric signs come on, and the red and green stop-and-go traffic-signal, and the crowd going by, and the horse-cabs clippety-clopping along the edge of the solid taxi traffic, and the *poules* going by" [*SAR*, p. 14]. He picks up Georgette Hobin, the prostitute with the bad teeth whom he takes dining and dancing.

Today's horse-cabs are cars, nobody notices traffic lights, the *poules* have moved, and the Napolitain is a chain steak house, the Hippopotame.

81. Au Nègre Joyeux

14, Rue Mouffetard
[5th; Monge]

Jake Barnes and Bill Gorton hear music coming from Au Nègre Joyeux as they stroll drunkenly through Paris. Only the sign remains today, a curiosity perched atop the modern Codec grocery store on the Place de la Contrescarpe.

82. *New York Herald Tribune* office

49, Avenue de l'Opéra
[2nd; Opéra]

Jake Barnes and Georgette Hobin pass by the *Tribune*'s "bureau with the window full of clocks" in *The Sun Also Rises*. A number of newspaper offices were once located near the Opéra; Jake Barnes's fictional office—complete with secretary and an elevator—was located two blocks away.

Cancelled portions of the novel reveal Barnes was wounded in 1916, met Brett in a British hospital, and returned to New York as a journalist. He started the Continental Press Association, which became "the third largest feature service" in America by 1920, when he moved to Paris as its European director. "When you have a title like that, translated into French on the letterheads, and only have to work about four or five hours a day and all the salary you want you are pretty well fixed" [Svoboda, p. 134].

Barnes's "work" consisted of rewriting stories from the French morning papers. Hemingway was not above this himself; several of his stories for the *Star* copy wire stories. He even copied himself, stringing for two wire services while working for the *Star*. In addition to color pieces on Paris, he covered several political conferences, saw Fascism firsthand in Italy, and covered the Greek retreat in 1922–23. He turned an article on the last into the war vignette preceding Chapter 2 of *In Our Time*.

83. Ney, Marshal Michel
Carrefour de l'Observatoire
[statue]
[6th; Port Royal]

Originally erected across the street near the wall where Ney was shot on December 7, 1815, his statue now stands in front of La Closerie de Lilas. Confidant to both Jake Barnes and Hemingway, Ney inspired Hemingway in *A Moveable Feast* to remain loyal to Gertrude Stein, "to serve her and see she gets justice for the good work she had done as long as I can, so help me God and Mike Ney. But the hell with her lost-generation talk and all the dirty, easy labels" [*AMF*, p. 31].

Formerly Napoleon's right-arm general, Marshal Michel Ney was sent by the restored monarchy to capture Napoleon after he escaped from Elba. Ney swore to return him to Paris in an iron cage. Instead, he knelt before his emperor and handed him an army of 60,000 men. They rode to defeat in Waterloo. The Royalist Chamber of Peers had him shot for his troubles.

He is buried in Paris's Père Lachaise cemetery. Or, if you believe the legend, in the Third Creek Presbyterian Church graveyard outside Cleveland, North Carolina, a town to which he supposedly escaped and where he died a schoolteacher. His marble tombstone reads: "In Memory of Peter Stewart Ney, a native of France, soldier of the French Revolution under Napoleon Bonaparte, who departed this life Nov 15th 1846 aged 77 years."

84. Café de la Paix
12, Boulevard des Capucines
[9th; Opéra]

One of Paris's largest cafés, the Paix wraps around an entire side of the busy Place de l'Opéra. The Paix seems to offer little to justify its 15-franc coffees and 25-franc beers, because you can see, smell, hear, feel, taste, and almost touch the diesel-spouting traffic while sitting on its terrace. Nevertheless, there are customers enough to keep men with Polaroids in business, each willing to snap your photo to prove to the folks back home that you really did pay these prices.

Hemingway and Hadley had dinner here their first Christmas in Paris. Afterwards, they discovered they couldn't pay the bill. Hemingway had to run across the Seine to their hotel for more money, leaving Hadley as hostage.

85. Le Pavillon du Lac Montsouris

29, Rue Gazan
[14th; Cité Universitaire]

Jake and Brett ride by this restaurant "where they have the pool of live trout and where you can sit and look out over the park" [*SAR*, p. 27]. The guidebooks also rave about Le Pavillon, Robert claiming, "*Une soirée au Pavillon du Lac est une soirée de province, une soirée de repos.*" In good weather, you can sit on the terrace and look out over a tree-lined lake, crowded with ducks being fed by the neighborhood children. Mothers stroll by with baby carriages, and old couples sit on park benches. On the periphery of old walled Paris, you think yourself in the country.

86. La Pêche Miraculeuse

Bas Meudon,
outside Paris

A fifteen-minute walk from Gare du Meudon, La Pêche Miraculeuse was served by steamboat in Hemingway's day. He and Hadley came to this well-known hotel and open-air restaurant to eat *les fritures de goujons* (fried fish). "It was a place out of a Maupassant story with a view over the river [Seine] as Sisley had painted it" [*AMF*, p. 44].

La Pêche Miraculeuse is in ruins today, the adjoining Haliope's Hôtel de la Pêche Mervailleuse's mosaic-lined facade hides squalid apartments, and the Sisley landscape embraces a Renault factory. Downriver, however, *la France profonde* beckons with riverside garden plots, moored barges, and fishermen.

Parisians still fish the Seine as they did in Hemingway's day, with "long, jointed cane poles . . . with very fine leaders and light gear and quill floats." The ends of the Îles de la Cité and St. Louis are the best spots to look for them as they fish the grass-choked back eddies for *goujon*, fingerling fish that Hemingway described as "plump and sweet-fleshed with a finer flavor than sardines even." You eat them bones and all, by the plateful, washing them down with white wine. Schoolfish, they are best caught by baiting the water; to clean them, you merely pinch their guts.

87. Pelletier et Caventou
[statue]

Place Louis Marin
[5th; Luxembourg]

Jake Barnes and Bill Gorton pass this monument to the "gentlemen who invented pharmacy" on their drunken stroll through Paris. In Hemingway's day there were "two men in flowing robes" [*SAR*, p. 72]. But the Germans filched the metal in World War II and now a half-nude stone woman—La Guerison—reclines here.

Pierre-Joseph Pelletier and Joseph-Blenamie Caventou discovered quinine in 1820 (at 45, Rue Jacob, though Hemingway probably didn't know the address). He had reason to thank them, however: in 1922 he caught malaria while covering the Greek-Turkish War and had to buy quinine pills to cure it.

5, Rue André Barsacq
88. La Petite Chaumière
[18th; Abbesses]

Hemingway consigns a "rotten son of a bitch" and his "dirty camping mouth" who interrupts his writing in *A Moveable Feast* to "the Petite Chaumiere where you belong" [*AMF*, p. 92]. Three doors from the Montmartre funicular, La Petite Chaumière was a notorious transvestite bar. Bayard claims it had "*une reputation équivoque,*" was often raided by the police, and was frequented by "*éléments pour la plupart de nationalité étrangère, préjudiciables à la renommée de la France*" (a questionable reputation . . . being frequented largely by foreigners who give France a bad name).

Hemingway's homophobia is now a popular topic, especially among the "methinks he doth protest too much" school of thought. But he was not alone in his bigotry; writing what he hoped would be a popular guidebook, in 1927 Reynolds described the Chaumière's patrons as "men of a certain degenerate tendency who infest every large city. . . . Freaks [who] cavort around and swish their skirts and sing in Falsetto" [pp. 194–95].

Hemingway's crude and Reynolds's cruder homophobia smack of voyeurism. In truth, Parisian tolerance for Lord Alfred Douglas's "love that dare not speak its name" was part of the City of Lights' allure, part of what made it for Hemingway the "super-Sodom and grander Gomorrah" of the West.

81, Boulevard St. Michel
89. Petit Taxidermist
[5th; Luxembourg]

Bill Gorton offers to buy Jake Barnes a stuffed dog at this taxidermist's. " 'Pretty stuffed dogs,' Bill said. 'Certainly brighten up your flat' " [*SAR*, p. 72].

This drunken offer is Hemingway's revenge on his impossible landlady, Madame Chautard, who lived beneath the Hemingways on Rue Notre-Dame-des-Champs. She was a "mad woman" inordinately fond of her pet dog. Finding it dead on the cobblestoned courtyard one morning, she accused one and all of having poisoned it, until an autopsy revealed the dog had been run over by a truck. She opted to stuff it.

Stuffing pets was not uncommon in France. Fellow expatriate Elliot Paul knew a taxidermist who specialized in the art of stuffing pets. M. Noel, Paul relates, took pleasure in "accentuating" the resemblances he found between owner and pet.

In addition to stuffing dogs, Parisians skinned cats, Paul notes. They then sold the fur, which was turned into mittens for the winter [Paul, pp. 6–7].

90. Picasso, Pablo   7, Rue des Grands Augustins
[apartment]   *[6th; St. Michel]*

When Hemingway stopped by to see Picasso during the liberation of Paris in August 1944, he was out. When the concierge suggested Hemingway leave a gift as had many others, he dropped off a case of grenades, scrawling "to Picasso from Hemingway" across its label [Gilot and Lake, p. 61].

After the war Mary Hemingway and Hemingway found Picasso at home. After touring his studio, they were presented with "the skeleton of a bicycle, with the handlebars turned forward. '*Mon taureau*,' Picasso said." Later, they dined with the Spaniard at his favorite restaurant, Le Catalan, at 16, Rue des Grands Augustins [Mary Hemingway, p. 117].

Picasso's apartment building is marked with a plaque. The street itself, narrow and lined with stone houses, is a breath of old Paris only minutes from Place St. Michel.

91. Place de la Contrescarpe   *[5th; Monge]*

What book-nourished Americans expect of the Left Bank, the Place de la Contrescarpe is a seedy, tree-shaded square lined with cafés, a *boulangerie*, *boucherie*, restaurants, a smattering of bums, and an *épicerie*.

Little has changed since Hemingway lived around the corner

Pablo Picasso's apartment.

and a drunk Jake Barnes stumbled across the square sixty years ago. The S bus no longer stops here, and Au Nègre Joyeux is closed, but its sign remains. The Café des Amateurs, now La Chope, still has "the long zinc bar" and is still crowded with "old men and women." Carved in stone over the *boucherie* and *restaurant chinois* is the legend, "Maison de la Pomme de Pin MCC," pretending to a drinking tradition as old as Rabelais.

Here Hemingway witnessed a Bastille Day party. Seated on

wine casks, an impromptu band of an accordion, bagpipe, two drums, and a cornet led a crowd of "shop girls, butchers, bakers, laborers, tram conductors and laundresses, and bookmakers" in a four-night revel, he told *Star* readers [*Dateline*, p. 183].

The colorful Rue Mouffetard starts here. Mouffetard's daily market, its stalls crowding onto the alley's cobblestones, is the same that Henry Miller raved over. The odors of fish, roasting chicken, bread, and stale beer mingle with the cries of fruit vendors; street signs for the *tabac*, *boucheries*, cobblers, and bakers crowd the view, and people from every continent crowd the steeply sloping alley.

92. Place Edmond Rostand   *[5th; Luxembourg]*

Jake Barnes breakfasted on brioche and coffee in a *Muirhead*-recommended café where the Free Time Hamburger stands today. Florists and law students still trudge by in the morning, and working stiffs still catch the bus for the Right Bank out front, but styrofoam cups and *"le hamburger"* reign here and across the street at McDonald's. The only remnant of this part of Hemingway's Paris is still called the Luxembourg Bar, but has crossed the street and lost its allure and appears in only a few tourist guides.

Hemingway's favorite S bus is defunct, its route split up. But buses remain a great way to see Paris. What cost Hemingway four cents will cost you four francs today.

93. Place St. Michel   *[5th; St. Michel]*

The busy crossroads of the Left Bank, today's Place St. Michel is hardly the place to write a short story. Yet Hemingway says in *A Moveable Feast* that he frequented a quiet café here, drinking *café au lait* and rum St. James as he wrote "The Three Day Blow." And who knows, perhaps the story's subterranean tension owes as much to the rums and an anonymous French "beauty . . . whoever you are" who chanced to sit opposite Hemingway as it does to the critics' preferred notions of a youthful love affair recollected in tranquility.

"Empty and both sad and happy as though I had made love," Hemingway feasts sensually after writing the story on "a dozen *portugaises* and a half-carafe of the dry white wine" [*AMF*, pp. 5–6]. The French are famous for their *huitres* (oysters)—the large, green, coppery *marennes* and fat, coppery *belons*, which Street says

Place St. Michel.

are "very expensive, costing in good restaurants from $1.20 to $1.60 per dozen" [Street, p. 191]. The smaller, cheaper *portugaise* is what Hemingway dined on when he paid the bill.

Today's *huitre*, farmed and bought in bulk, comes with a certificate of health. It is also liable to be the spawn of oriental species, quicker and hence cheaper to produce.

94. Polidor's

41, Rue Monsieur le Prince
[6th; Luxembourg]

Although Hemingway never mentions dining here, this *crémerie*-restaurant's former owner and manager Madame Marie-Christine K'Vella swears he did. And a host of other literary luminaries including Joyce and Valery did sign Polidor's *livre d'or*. With small wooden tables crowded together under the pressed tin ceiling, butcher's paper tablecloths, and handwritten menus, Polidor's retains much of the flavor of the twenties. Its moderately priced menu is traditional and unvarying—guinea, chicken, snails. The best wine buy here is Cahors, Hemingway's favorite.

A must is the caramelized *tarte aux pommes*. Inches-thick slices are served hot, drowning in cream. French apple pies beat Mom's for taste and variety. There is Polidor's open-faced *tarte aux pommes*, the upside-down *tarte Tatine*, supposedly invented by two old maids who turned a baking disaster into a treat, and the wrapped-up *chausson aux pommes*. Most beautiful is the open-faced pie, whose slices of apples spiral round its center like a snail's shell.

Discovered by an American tourists' guide, K'Vella raked in enough money in three years to sell out. The new owner, however, has promised to change neither the menu nor the prices.

Public Baths

95. Pont de Sully   *[5th; Sully Morland]*

Neither of Hemingway's first two apartments had baths (or private toilets, for that matter). So he and Hadley used the public baths, of which there were—and still are—plenty in Paris. He preferred the cold-water "public bath-house down at the foot of the street [Cardinal Lemoine] by the river" *[AMF,* p. 40]. Open May 1 to September 30, the Seine bathhouses were "colder than the Maine coast," he wrote Ernest Walsh in 1925 *[Letters,* p. 169].

Paris boasted nine cold-water bathhouses along the Seine in 1925. The closest to Rue du Cardinal Lemoine was next to the Pont de Sully. Nearer the Hemingways at 63, Rue du Cardinal Lemoine and 42, Rue des Fosses St. Bernard was a former Turkish bathhouse, the Cardinal Lemoine, run by Mlle. Aubry.

96. Pont de la Tournelle   *[4th; Pont Marie]*

Stopping here on his drunken stroll through Paris with Jake Barnes, Bill Gorton looks downriver towards Notre Dame and exclaims, "It's pretty grand. . . . God, I love to get back." Although *The Sun Also Rises* describes the men as standing on "the wooden foot-bridge" *[SAR,* p. 77], there hasn't been a wooden bridge in this location for centuries. The stone Pont de la Tournelle was being repaired from 1923 to 1928; Hemingway's reference is to a temporary structure.

97. Porte Maillot   *[17th; Porte Maillot]*

Hemingway wrote his father on May 2, 1922, that "May day was quiet here although the Comrades shot a couple of policemen"

[*Letters*, p. 66]. In an unpublished piece, he claims to have watched police with swords charge demonstrators at the Porte Maillot. A sixteen-year-old "who looked like a prep school quarter back" shot two of the police [Baker, *Ernest Hemingway*, p. 90].

The worst had been feared for May Day 1922. The French had called up reinforcements, bought newfangled radio cars, and even put up an observation plane. However, the *New York Times* reported "the quietest May Day known in Paris for several years. The fact is the bottom has dropped out of Bolshevism and Communism in France." The only arrests reported were two striking streetcar employees, the only violence that a reporter slapped the chief of the Communist party. But when did Hemingway ever let the facts stand in the way of a good story?

98. Pound, Ezra　　　　　　　　70 bis, Rue Notre-Dame-
[apartment]　　　　　　　　　　des-Champs　*[6th; Vavin]*

Down the street from Hemingway's sawmill apartment, Pound's interior apartment here looked out into the courtyard. "As poor as Gertrude Stein's studio was rich," Pound's was hung with Dorothy Pound's and Japanese paintings, and photos of vorticist Gaudier-Brzeska's work and his head of Pound.

Pound taught Hemingway "to distrust adjectives," and Hemingway taught Pound to box. They were sparring in Pound's studio the day Wyndam Lewis walked in, dressed "like someone out of *La Bohème*" [*AMF*, pp. 107–9]. He reminded Hemingway of "toe-jam." *A Moveable Feast*'s distaste for Lewis stems in part from Lewis's 1934 attack in "The Dumb Ox" on Hemingway's "Stein stutter." When Hemingway first read this piece in Shakespeare and Company, he broke Beach's flower vase.

Hemingway also met Ernest Walsh at Pound's. Walsh's *This Quarter* published "Big Two-Hearted River" and "The Undefeated" in 1925. Walsh arrived with two mink-draped young lovelies, one of whom confided to Hemingway that Walsh got $1,200 a poem from Harriet Monroe's *Poetry* which was, she cooed, "more than Eddie Guest gets" [*AMF*, p. 123].

Pound is one of the few expatriates Hemingway does not attack in *A Moveable Feast*. He praises him as "kinder and more Christian than I was." Pound was "irascible but so perhaps have been many saints." While Hemingway was writing the book, Pound was still confined as criminally insane to St. Elizabeths in Washington, D.C. Hemingway, working for his saint's release, conceded, "Pound's crazy. All poets are. . . . They have to be. You don't put a poet like Pound in the loony bin. For history's sake we shouldn't keep him there" [Baker, *Ernest Hemingway*, p. 539].

99. Café Pré aux Clercs
31, Rue Jacob and 30, Rue Bonaparte
[6th; St. Germain des Prés]

Hemingway's favorite restaurant his first year in Paris, the Pré aux Clercs got a rave review in the *Star*. For fifty cents each, he and Hadley got dinners equal "to the best restaurants in America." Thick steaks and potatoes were 2.40 francs, red wine 60 centimes the bottle, and beer 40 centimes the glass [*Dateline*, p. 89]. Today's coffee costs more than a Hemingway meal.

Not in today's guidebooks, the Pré aux Clercs made those of the twenties. Robert praised it as "*une maison sympathique*," with a "*cuisine honnête, forte bonne.*" Popular with painters, writers, and students, it was half a block from the expatriate mecca, the Hôtel d'Angleterre.

100. Prunier's
9, Rue Duphot
[1st; Madeleine]

A temple of seafood according to Gault-Millau, Prunier's had been a legend for forty-five years before Hemingway and Hadley blew their track winnings here in 1922 on "oysters and *crabe Mexicaine* with glasses of Sancerre" [*AMF*, p. 53]. Years later, a richer Papa ate here with Mary Hemingway and Marlene Dietrich.

Luck at the tracks helps if Prunier's tempts you; *à la carte* prices began at 250 francs in 1987. When Alfred Prunier opened his oyster shop in 1877, the French ignored him; only the English and Americans ate oysters then, Street says. An anonymous American showed Prunier how to make oyster pan stew, thus inaugurating cooking at Prunier's. So popular was Prunier's with expatriates in the twenties that Emile Prunier planted beds of Cape Cod clams and Blue Point oysters for the homesick.

101. La Quatrième République
42, Rue Jacob
[6th; St. Germain des Prés]

Opened by disgruntled socialist M. Chuzeville during the Third Republic, the Fourth Republic Restaurant looked forward to the dawn of a new political era. Painted by soon-to-be-famous Rus-

sian Hoyningen-Huene in avant garde *trompe l'oeil,* the Fourth
Republic was Janet Flanner's favorite restaurant and the setting
for a Hemingway Christmas story in the *Star.* Renamed the Restaurant of the Third Republic, La Quatrième served two homesick
Americans their first Christmas meal away from home. It was a
gristly turkey cut in squares *sans* cranberries, and the dessert was
burned. "I didn't know Paris was like this," the girl said. "The boy
put his arm around her. At least that was one thing you could do
in a Parisian restaurant. . . . You do not know what Christmas is
until you lose it in some foreign land" [*Dateline,* pp. 425–26].

Hemingway and Hadley had lost their first Paris Christmas
too. Only their disaster occurred at the Café de la Paix and was
financial, not culinary.

The restaurant Il Casanova stands here today. The same narrow steps that Flanner said tripped waiters as well as customers
lead upstairs to the small room Hemingway remembered. But no
one remembered Le Quatrième Republique the day I ate there.

102. Café la Régence
161, Rue St. Honoré
[1st; Palais Royal]

Hemingway told his 1934 *Esquire* readers that he had discovered
"natural champagne" on draft here for "nine francs a wooden
pitcher" [*Byline,* p. 156]. Which he proceeded to drink in this
café, where Napoleon played chess when he was First Consul.
Unfortunately, the Régence is now a tourist agency.

103. Au Rendezvous des Mariners
33, Quai d'Anjou
[4th; Pont Marie]

Now a private residence, Madame Lecomte's celebrated restaurant
fed a Jake Barnes and Bill Gorton disgruntled by their forty-five-
minute wait occasioned by the "discovery" of the Rendezvous by
the American Women's Club tour guide. Gorton had discovered
Lecomte's during World War I.

The American Women's Club was not alone in being charmed
by Lecomte's "quaint" establishment. Street says it was popular
with expatriates who promised visitors " 'a queer little place, very
French.' " And Robert waxed euphoric over its *"décor amusant,
petits tables de marbre ou de bois, nappes de papier"* (amusing decor,
marble or wooden tables, paper tablecloths).

The Rendezvous was popular with boatmen, Street notes, who
once a year elected a king and fêted him here.

Hôtel Ritz, back entrance; Bar Hemingway is to the
right, inside.

                                            15, Place Vendôme
104. Hôtel Ritz   *[1st; Opéra]*
Hemingway could not afford even a drink at the world's most
famous hotel when he first came to Paris. But Papa could, and it
was Papa and his band of *maquis* who liberated the Ritz's cellar in
August 1944. "Dirty and dusty, in berets, undershirts, and grease-
stained blue-denim work clothes," they crowded into the posh
lobby, where Hemingway promptly ordered "seventy-three dry
martinis" [Collins and Lapierre, pp. 325–26].

Billeted in room 31, Hemingway used to spend most nights in room 86 with Mary Walsh. Here he proposed to her: "Will you marry me, Pickle? Will you, Mary Walsh, take me, Ernest Hemingway, for thy lawful husband?" [Mary Hemingway, p. 166]. He knew the line well; she would be his fourth wife.

Living down the hall from Mary, Marlene Dietrich used to sit on Hemingway's tub and sing to him while he shaved. Dietrich gave the couple her double bed as a Christmas gift; unfortunately, it was infested with mites. It was in room 31 that Hemingway, given a brace of German pistols, dropped a photo of Mary and Noel Monks into the toilet and shot six bullets into it—destroying the then hard-to-replace toilet and plumbing.

Papa's favorite Paris bar was the small one to the right of the Ritz's back door at 38, Rue Cambon. Now the Bar Hemingway, it is a shrine to Hemingway, with photos on the wall and his bust on the bar. The last staff member to remember Papa retired several years ago, according to the bartender. But the Ritz's restaurant, l'Espadon, remembers Papa with its "*homard à la broche Hemingway.*" For those with more in common with young Hemingway than Papa—beware; the *à la carte* menu here will cost you 500 to 600 francs.

In 1956, while staying in rooms 56 and 57, Hemingway was presented with two suitcases filled with "a dozen or more blue and yellow notebooks handwritten mostly in pencil and hundreds of pages of typed stories and sketches." He had left them with the hotel in 1927; they became the basis for *A Moveable Feast.*

Mary Hemingway says they stayed in yet another room, room 36, when they visited the hotel in 1953.

105. Rohrbach, Maria   10 bis, Avenue des Gobelins
[apartment]   *[5th; Gobelins]*

Mr. Bumby's nursemaid Maria lived here. She worked for the Hemingways when they lived over the sawmill and kept Bumby during their trip to Pamplona. During World War II, Hemingway's *maquis* sang the song Bumby had memorized in case he were ever lost in Paris:

Dix bis Avenue des Gobelins,
Dix BIS Avenue des GOBELINS,
DIX BIS AVENUE DES GOBELINS,
THAT'S WHERE MY BUMBY LIVES.

Café de la Rotonde.

106. **Café de la Rotonde**

103, Boulevard du Montparnasse
[6th; Vavin]

"No matter what cafe in Montparnasse you ask a taxi-driver to bring you to from the right bank of the river, they always take you to the Rotonde," Jake says in *The Sun Also Rises* [*SAR*, p. 42]. The Rotonde's clientele were "the scum of Greenwich Village. . . . They have all striven so hard for a careless individuality of clothing that they have achieved a sort of uniformity of eccentricity. . . . You can find anything you are looking for at the Rotonde

—except serious artists," Hemingway told his *Star* readers [*Dateline*, pp. 114–15]. The Rotonde advertised in Bottin as having "*le dancing le plus gai et le plus curieux de Paris.*"

Celebrated for its own art gallery, the Rotonde served the likes of Apollinaire, Picasso, Max Jacob, and Modigliani. Still popular with foreigners, the Rotonde's prices are as elevated as those of its neighbors. It offers a 41-franc "cocktail rotonde"—a mix of Campari, Martini, and champagne.

107. St. Honoré d'Eylau
9, Place Victor Hugo
[16th; Victor Hugo]

Hemingway married Pauline Pfeiffer here May 10, 1927, in a Catholic ceremony made possible by his having renounced his Protestant marriage to Hadley. When the Catholics demanded proof of his baptism in the faith, Hemingway recollected having been blessed by a priest while lying in an Italian dressing station during World War I. This and the marriage stuck in the craw of some of his friends; Ada MacLeish threw the newlyweds a lunch but failed to attend the service.

A fervent Catholic, Pfeiffer tried to get Hemingway to convince Hadley to convert Bumby. Hadley, remembering Hemingway on his knees in church only twice—once at their wedding and once at Bumby's baptism—replied that the Episcopal Church in which he had been baptized was good enough.

108. St. Joseph des Carmes
70, Rue de Vaugirard
[6th; St. Sulpice]

An impotent newlywed, Hemingway discovered here that the age of miracles lives yet. Whether living out his guilt over Hadley or his fantasies about Jake Barnes, he "was in a hell of a jam" with Pauline. After he had submitted uselessly to electric shocks and calves-liver cocktails, Pauline suggested he pray. Hemingway ran round the corner to this Baroque church, prayed, and returned to the Rue Férou apartment, where "we made love like we had invented it. We never had any trouble again. That's when I became a Catholic" [Hotchner, p. 51].

109. St. Luke's Chapel
5, Rue de la Grande Chaumière
[6th; Vavin]

Bumby was baptized an Episcopalian here, with Jewish Gertrude Stein as godmother and a Catholic godfather. Where the chapel

St. Sulpice.

stood is now part of Reid Hall, a center for several American colleges, which may be entered at 4, Rue de Chevreuse. The concierge swears a small classroom in back, La Maison Verte, is the chapel, but center officials believe it to have been razed.

Place St. Sulpice
110. St. Sulpice   *[6th; St. Sulpice]*

Down the street from Rue Férou, St. Sulpice saw Hemingway and Pauline attend religiously its Sunday mass before he headed for the races. In *A Moveable Feast*, he describes the quiet square with its "fountain with lions, and pigeons walk[ing] on the pavement and perch[ing] on the statues of the bishops" [*AMF*, pp. 69–70]. The four bishops are "*les quatre points cardinals*," a pun on their facing the four points of the compass, as none became a cardinal.

99, Boulevard du Montparnasse
III. **Café Le Select**   [6th; Vavin]

Jake Barnes and Robert Cohn meet Harvey Stone here. "He had a pile of saucers in front of him, and he needed a shave" [*SAR*, p. 42]. Stone is Hemingway's little-disguised version of Harold

Café le Select.

Stearns, the American expatriate who had edited *America and the Young Intellectual*, in which he lambasted philistine American culture. Preferring Europe, he wound up as a barfly in Montparnasse, making ends meet by writing a racing column, "Peter Pickem," for the Paris *Chicago Tribune*. Jake and Hemingway liked Stone, the latter perhaps because Stone favored him with racing tips. And Stearns liked Hemingway; "he has always acted as you would expect a friend to act," he recalled years later [Stearns, pp. 357–58]. Stearns also claimed he convinced Liveright to accept *In Our Time* for publication.

Frances Clyne is vouchsafed in the Select a vision of Cohn's reasons for dumping her: "Someday they'll put a tablet up. Like at Lourdes. . . . Robert's always wanted to have a mistress, and if he doesn't marry me, why, then he's had one" [*SAR*, p. 51]. Jake sneaks out by the side door on the Rue Vavin.

112. Shakespeare and Company

12, Rue de l'Odéon
[6th; Odéon]

Sylvia Beach's English-language bookstore is probably the most famous Parisian literary landmark for Americans. Today's store is on the Seine; in Hemingway's day, it was by the Luxembourg Gardens, much nearer the heart of the expatriate community.

Beach's ledger for December 28, 1921, indicates Hemingway paid 12 francs for the right to check out two volumes at a time from her lending library. In *A Moveable Feast*, he remembers taking four home.

Beach, who had published Joyce's *Ulysses* in 1922 ("paper bound, printed on poor paper, it abounded in typographical errors" and sold for 60 francs, Laney says), fell afoul of the Depression. When their remittance checks stopped, the expatriates returned to America, leaving her with no clientele and less money. Hemingway gave a public reading May 12, 1937, at her store to raise money.

Beach modeled her store on that of her lover, Adrienne Monnier. Monnier's La Maison des Amis des Livres, across the street at number 7, drew such French writers as Gide, Claudel, Larbaud, and Valery. Monnier was the first person to publish Hemingway in French.

Shakespeare and Company closed during World War II. A German officer threatened to confiscate it when Beach refused to sell

Shakespeare and Company bookstore today. *(Photograph by Deborah Wong)*

him her last copy of *Finnegans Wake*. Hours after he had stormed out, she had hidden all her books and even painted over the shop sign.

George Whitman opened today's version of Shakespeare and Company (37, Rue de la Bucherie) in 1951 as Le Mistral, changing the name in 1964. Most popular with the "Beats," Whitman's store remains a cultural center today. Upstairs at Shakespeare and Company is a visiting writers' room and a collection of Beach memorabilia. Whitman's Sunday afternoon tea—by invitation—may bring you face to face with established and struggling artists.

113. The Sign of the Black Manikin Press　　　**4, Rue Delambre**
**　**　　　　　　　　　　　　　　　　　　　*[14th; Vavin]*
Edward Titus, husband to Helena Rubenstein, opened a bookstore here in 1924. His Black Manikin Press took over Ernest Walsh's *This Quarter*, which had published Hemingway's short stories. Titus published Kiki's memoirs in 1930. Kiki (Alice Prin)

was Man Ray's much-photographed mistress and a Montparnasse fixture and symbol. Hemingway wrote the introduction to her book.

In the 1955 edition, Kiki and her companion, a dead fish (I kid you not), find Hemingway at the Waldorf Astoria in New York. After he has made sure the fish is comfortably iced down, she tells him, "Well, it is said by some in Paris that if I had not let you write that introduction to my *Memoires* you would probably be polishing spitoons in some minor hangout in Montparnasse."

Hemingway replies, "Did you know, Kiki, that there are people in town who say but for that introduction which you *begged* me to write you might still be warming beds for minor French artists at five francs a night?" [Kiki, p. 108].

Kiki remembered young Hemingway resembled "a first-communion lad"; she wondered if he were still a virgin [Meyer, p. 66].

114. Square Louvois [2nd, Bourse]

In *A Moveable Feast*, Hemingway mentions eating at a restaurant on this quiet square across from the Bibliothèque Nationale. A number of restaurants came and went here during the twenties, the most durable of which was M. Marie's at 4, Rue Louvois. Today's cafés, located on the other side of the square on Rue Rameau, have no Hemingway connection. The square itself is a welcome spot of green in Paris; its fountain is almost noisy enough to drown out the cars.

115. Stade Yves-du-Manoir Colombes, *outside Paris*

Hemingway was one of a few thousand Americans and almost no Frenchmen who watched the New York Giants whip the Chicago White Sox 8–0 on November 8, 1924, in an exhibition game here. The then-new Olympic stadium was too small for baseball, and home runs slammed into the stands counted as two base hits, the *New York Times* reported. The few befuddled French who showed up never figured out the difference between balls and strikes. Unimpressed by baseball's *haute couture*, a Paris paper compared unfavorably the Giants' uniforms to those of convicts. "Kill the umpire," garbled in translation and retranslation, became "Death to the arbiter."

Gertrude Stein's apartment.

116. Stein, Gertrude 27, Rue de Fleurus
[apartment] *[6th; St. Placide]*

Stein and her lover Alice B. Toklas lived here for nearly thirty years. Stein's studio and apartment was an expatriate center; Hemingway remembers in *A Moveable Feast* his and Hadley's visits to what was like "one of the best rooms in the finest museum except that there was a big fireplace and . . . they gave you good things to eat and tea and natural distilled liqueurs made from purple plums, yellow plums or wild raspberries" [*AMF*, pp. 13–14]. While Toklas entertained Hadley, Stein and Hemingway talked literature.

Stein popularized the phrase "*une génération perdue*" that Hemingway used in *The Sun Also Rises*. According to him, she got it from a garage owner who was cursing his veteran mechanic.

In *A Moveable Feast*, Hemingway praises Stein's "rhythms and the uses of words in repetition." He parodies this style in *For Whom the Bell Tolls*, where Robert Jordan spoofs Stein's famous "A rose is a rose is a rose," with "A rose is a rose is an onion. . . . An onion is an onion is an onion . . . a stone is a stein is a rock is a boulder is a pebble" [*FBT*, p. 289].

This parody came after Hemingway and Stein had fallen out. Toklas claimed she had talked Stein into dumping Hemingway. Toklas had tired of Hemingway's obsession with "*le legend, toujours le legend*" [Simon, p. 118]; it had been she, she said, who introduced him to Pamplona, which he promptly ruined for her.

Stein's *Autobiography of Alice B. Toklas* may have played a role too. It labels Hemingway as yellow and "ninety percent Rotarian." Whatever the reasons, Hemingway took his revenge in *A Moveable Feast*. Again parodying Stein's "uses of words in repetition," he overhears her talking to Toklas, "Don't, pussy. Don't. Don't, please don't. Please don't, pussy" [*AMF*, p. 118].

According to Hemingway, Stein had tried to educate him about homosexuality. Claiming that sodomy drives males to "drink and take drugs," she said "In women it is the opposite. They do nothing that they are disgusted by and nothing that is repulsive and afterwards they are happy and they can lead happy lives together" [*AMF*, pp. 19–20].

117. Studio-Apartments Hôtel
9, Rue Delambre
[14th; Vavin]

Lady Duff Twysden wrote Hemingway a note on stationery from this hotel in 1925 pleading for 3,000 francs to help her out of "a stinking fix." Hemingway's response is unknown. Across the street from The Dingo Bar, this is perhaps the same hotel Brett Ashley and Mike Campbell stay in in *The Sun Also Rises*. " '*I* believe it's a brothel,' Mike said. 'And *I* should know' " [*SAR*, p. 83]. Still a rooming house, the hotel has a twenties-looking ironwork facade.

118. Tennis Courts
63, Boulevard Arago
[13th; Denfert Rochereau]

Still here are the red clay tennis courts on which Hemingway, Pound, Loeb, and Williams played in the twenties. "Ernest's game was not too good," Loeb recalled [Loeb, p. 194].

The courts are three doors from the grim walled Prison de la Santé, where the guillotine is kept. Hemingway's *Star* readers learned the intricacies of French executions from him. The condemned prisoner learned that he was to die only an hour before his daybreak execution. After a cigarette and glass of rum, his neck was shaved. He was marched outside the prison gates to the waiting crowd and guillotine [*Dateline*, p. 121].

The public executioner in Hemingway's day was Anatole François Deibler, "the most feared man in France." A third-generation executioner, Deibler died of a heart attack at the Métro stop Porte de St. Cloud in February 1939 on the way to his 301st execution, according to Janet Flanner. In memory of Marie Antoinette, "*La Veuve* Capet," the guillotine is called "the widow." The executioner is called Monsieur de Paris, his assistants Les Valets. The Deiblers, Flanner says, actually owned the guillotine, keeping the seven-kilo blade packed in Vaseline between uses. Made in Langrés, the French cutlery center, it never needed honing.

The French have recently outlawed executions. But the curious can still gawk at *la guillotine's* surprisingly thick *couperet* on display in La Conciergerie, the Île de la Cité's infamous Revolutionary prison.

119. Thomson, Virgil
[apartment]
17, Quai Voltaire
[7th; Pont Neuf]

American composer Virgil Thomson lived in a fifth-floor studio here from 1927 to 1940. He collaborated with Stein on *Four Saints in Three Acts* soon after his arrival. Thomson also scored *The Spanish Earth*, Hemingway's 1937 documentary on the Republic. He did not care for Hemingway, who "was part of a Montparnasse hard-liquor set, which, though thoroughly fascinated by itself, was less interesting to people not also drinking hard liquor" [Thomson, p. 110].

Thomson claims Stein got her "*une génération perdue*" from a French hotel manager. Stein meant it to imply the war had made the veterans "permanently rootless." Thomson points out that Hemingway, who returned to reporting after the war, "was not at all lost." In any case, if it had meant lost, Thomson, claims, someone got it wrong; the correct French would read *"une génération* de *perdus"* [Thomson, p. 50].

29, Quai d'Anjou
120. **Three Mountains Press**   *[4th; Pont Marie]*

William Bird's Three Mountains Press (named after the Parisian mountains Montparnasse, Montmartre, and Ste. Geneviève) published Hemingway's *in our time* at Christmas 1924. The limited edition (220 copies) contained the vignettes that appear in the longer *In Our Time*. Edmund Wilson praised its "artistic integrity," claiming its bullfight passages worthy of Goya [Baker, *Ernest Hemingway*, p. 134]. Others were less impressed; Mencken's *American Mercury* panned it as "written in the bad bold style of the Cafe Dôme"; the longer *In Our Time* was "Art On Its Last Legs," Henry Seidel Canby wrote [Callaghan, pp. 37–38].

Robert McAlmon's Contact Editions shared offices with Bird. McAlmon, whose fortuitous marriage to and divorce from an English heiress prompted wags to nickname him "Robber McAlimony," had printed Hemingway's *Three Stories and Ten Poems* in 1923.

Ford Madox Ford also ran his *transatlantic review* from here. Ford recalled they all "believed, I don't know why, that salvation could be found in leaving out capitals" [Ford, pp. 247–49]. Hemingway later termed the idea silly and affected. Hemingway was manuscript scout for the *review*, which he convinced to publish Stein's monumental *The Making of Americans.*

Ford held Thursday literary teas in the office. At one, Loeb first met a shabbily dressed Hemingway, whom he took afterward to Lavigne's Nègre de Toulouse for lobster and wine.

Though the presses have long since folded, the building that housed them remains.

40, Rue Fabert
121. *transition*   *[7th; Invalides]*

Eugene Jolas and Elliot Paul began *transition* in 1926 in room 16 on the fourth floor of a hotel here. The magazine published most of the expatriate luminaries, including Hemingway, Joyce, Dos Passos, MacLeish, Williams, Miller, and Stein. Laney recalls that few could understand what Stein and Joyce were writing. On one occasion, *transition* published Stein's "Essay on Composition as Explanation," accidentally shuffling the pages. "Neither they nor anyone else noticed it. Nobody, that is, except Miss Stein" [Laney, pp. 154–55].

Today used as apartments, the rooms of this former hotel look out on the spacious Esplanade des Invalides, among whose trees Parisians play *boules* and along whose avenues the Garde Republicainne escorts visiting dignitaries.

[NOTE: Morton gives address as "40 ter."]

122. Travellers' Club

25, Avenue des Champs-Elysées
[8th; Franklin D. Roosevelt]

Hemingway's rumored liberation of this private club during World War II amounted to little more than a complimentary bottle of champagne he cadged from the club president.

The club occupies the former Hôtel Paiva. Completed in 1866, the Paiva was Russian-born Thérèse Lachmann's bid for acceptance into Second Empire society. Her bed-hopping up the Paris social ladder having occurred after theirs, the Empire's collection of *parvenus* and *nouveaux riches* scorned her.

123. Trois et As Bar

Rue de Tournon
[6th; Rennes]

Loeb and Lady Duff Twysden held their first rendezvous in a "quiet place in paneled oak with English hunting scenes on the wall" on the Rue de Tournon near Foyot's, away from the Montparnasse gossips [Loeb, pp. 253–54]. A young English barman from whom Duff habitually borrowed money served them. This sounds like Jimmie Charters, who seems to have been barman in every Parisian bar.

Loeb does not name the bar he met Duff in, but in *This Must Be the Place*, Charters recalls working in the Trois et As Bar on Rue de Tournon. The expatriates soon discovered it; Charters remembers Pat Guthrie dancing the Highland fling and Edna St. Vincent Millay hearing the first of many "bull and fish stories" from Hemingway during *corrida* night here. McAlmon remembers that Hadley ran into Hemingway and Pauline here soon after her divorce. It was then, he says, the expatriate crowd learned of Hemingway's Catholic insistence on making his first marriage null. "All right, then, the child [Bumby] is altogether mine," Hadley told him [McAlmon, p. 346].

Just where the Trois et As was on the Rue de Tournon is unclear. Charters said that it was associated with a hotel. Perhaps it was located in the Hôtel de Londres et de Russie at 27—at least the name would explain the bar's English motif.

124. Vélodrome d'Hiver
8, Quai de Grennelle
[16th; Bir Hakim]

Replaced by a block of modern buildings in 1959, the "Vel' d'Hiv" was a favorite haunt of Hemingway. He recalled in *A Moveable Feast* its "high-banked wooden track and the whirring sound the tires made on the wood as the riders passed" during the Six Jours races he dragged both Hadley and Pauline to [*AMF*, p. 64]. Kiley remembers Hemingway's slugging it out with two thugs one night, to the delight of two American girls awed to be in the presence of a real author.

The Nazis used the 1910 enclosed track as a collection center July 16–17, 1942 when they deported over 13,000 Jews to Auschwitz. A plaque marks the place.

125. Vélodrome du Parc des Princes
Porte de St. Cloud
[16th; Porte de St. Cloud]

A new 50,000-seat soccer stadium replaces "the wickedest track of all," 660 meters of cement on which Hemingway saw "that great rider Ganay fall and heard his skull crumple" like a hard-boiled egg [*AMF*, p. 65]. Gustave Ganay, a champion in motor-paced bicycle races, died August 23, 1926, the day after his crash.

126. Hôtel Venitia
[Hemingway's room]
159, Boulevard du Montparnasse
[6th; Vavin]

Now closed, the Venitia was a scene of Hemingway's adulterous affair with Pauline Pfeiffer in 1926. Hadley and Bumby were waiting for him in Austria. He stayed at the Venitia on his way to New York to switch publishers. On his return, he passed up three trains from the Gare de l'Est so he could see Pauline, who lived on the Rue Picot (number unknown).

127. Café de Versailles

71, Rue de Rennes and
3, Place du 18 Juin 1940
[6th; Montparnasse Bienvenue]

Cohn kicked Barnes under the table here after he mentioned in front of Clyne their possibly visiting a girl in Strasbourg. They were drinking *fines* and coffee.

The Versailles, so named because one caught the train to Versailles from the Montparnasse station across the square, was described in Robert's 1925 guidebook as a good place to eat. Robert lamented, however, "*le passage des jolies filles qui s'ent vont au dancing célèbre caché dans le fond au bout d'un mystérieux couloir*" (the passing of young girls on their way to a famous dance club hidden at the end of a mysterious hallway). Street explains that the Versailles had a billiards parlor and dance club in back.

The view has changed drastically since Hemingway's day. Now Chez Hanzi Brasserie Alsacienne—open until 3:00 A.M.—looks out on the Tour du Montparnasse. Robert's "*jolies filles*" are elsewhere, although street rumor has it that gigolos rendezvous with older women at a nearby café.

128. Vetzel's Brasserie

1, Place de l'Opéra and Rue Auber
[9th; Opéra]

Barnes and Cohn have "hors d'oeuvres and beer" here, Cohn pumping Barnes for information about Brett. Cohn nearly slugs Barnes for calling Brett a drunk who's going to marry for money [*SAR*, p. 38]. This hangout of newsmen was long ago gobbled up by the Café de la Paix.

129. Les Vikings

29, Rue Vavin
[6th; Vavin]

In *A Moveable Feast*, Jules Pascin and his two prostitutes invite Hemingway to eat with them here. Specializing in Scandinavian food and beer, Vikings' second-floor "small compartments with curtains that can be discretely drawn" attracted a clientele interested in more than merely eating out, according to Street.

Pascin, Bulgarian-born painter of prostitutes, hanged himself in 1930. Eulogizing him, Hemingway wrote "They say the seeds of what we will do are in all of us, but it always seemed to me that in those who make jokes in life the seeds are covered with better soil and with a higher grade of manure" [*AMF*, p. 104].

Les Vikings is today a cafeteria.

130. Café-Restaurant Voltaire

1, Place de l'Odéon
[6th; Odéon]

Now gone, the Voltaire was once the haunt of the Encyclopedists and later Mallarmé, Gide, and Verlaine as well as senators and professors from the Luxembourg and Sorbonne.

Hemingway and American poet Allen Tate came here after meeting in Shakespeare and Company. They fell out over vermouth cassis debating Tate's opinion that Hemingway owed a lot to novelists Frederick Marryat and Daniel Defoe. Tate later concluded that Hemingway was a "complete son of a bitch" [Tate, pp. 59–60].

131. Hôtel Waldorf Florida

12, Boulevard Malesherbes
[8th; Madeleine]

Today's three-star Waldorf Florida had been commandeered by the YMCA when Hemingway stayed here for about a week in 1918 on his way to the Italian front. He wrote his parents, "have seen all the sights, the Champs Elysees, the Tuileries and the Arc de Triumph [sic] and so on. . . . Tonight we went to the Folies Bergere [illegible] ye straight and narrow for me" [Griffin, p. 64].

"Ye straight and narrow" is not the wartime Paris Hemingway recalled in *Torrents of Spring*. There he recounts an evening of sex with an anonymous but beautiful woman. Later on, he discovers they were part of a peep show.

132. Zelli's

16 bis, Rue Fontaine
[9th; Blanche]

Jake, Brett, and Count Mippipopolous wind up at this popular nightclub in *The Sun Also Rises*. "Perhaps the best known Night Resort in Paris," according to Reynolds, Zelli's was "the place to meet the people who came over on the boat with you" [Reynolds, p. 149]. Packed with " 'Hostesses' and 'Gigolos,' " Zelli's gave a simulacrum of Parisian decadence but was, Laney maintains, "no better than the other tourist traps" and "had the exact look of any night club in New York or London or Shanghai or Berlin" [Laney, pp. 193–95].

Mippipopolous disappears from *The Sun Also Rises* surrounded by three of Zelli's "hostesses," whose function was to seduce patrons into buying more and more champagne. Who he was modeled after in real life is unclear; Hadley claimed Hemingway invented the Count, but Charters guessed he might have been the lover of Greek art student, Mitzy. Mitzy, the model for *The Sun Also Rises'* Zizi (argot for penis), said his lover was unbelievably formal, insisting they shake hands with each other after they hopped in bed and turned out the light.

Zelli's folded long ago; today 16 bis is a doorway leading into an apartment building.

2

WALKING TOURS

The only real way to learn about Hemingway's Paris is to walk it as he did. The Métro reduces Paris to a series of unrelated stops; a taxi is too expensive. And, while a bus remains the best way to see large sections of the city, the flavor of the various quarters is best captured by walking them. In both *The Sun Also Rises* and *A Moveable Feast* Hemingway describes several walks that you can still take, following Jake Barnes and his creator around Paris. The following walks are designed to pass by the more prominent Hemingway sites in selected quarters. Less prominent sites, when nearby, are listed as optional sidetracks. For fuller descriptions of the places mentioned in the walks, use the number in brackets to find the entry in the Guide. A *Guide Michelin* or similar book will provide information on sites you pass not necessarily connected with Hemingway. No walk should take more than half a day. The energetic tourist can combine several tours into one if so inclined. All walks include cafés, bars, and public parks that may be used as resting places.

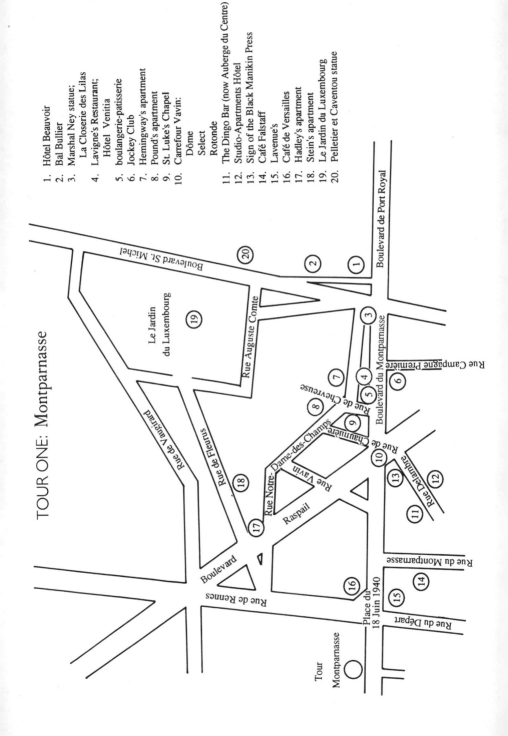

TOUR ONE: Montparnasse

1. Hôtel Beauvoir
2. Bal Bullier
3. Marshal Ney statue;
   La Closerie des Lilas
4. Lavigne's Restaurant;
   Hôtel Venitia
5. boulangerie-patisserie
6. Jockey Club
7. Hemingway's apartment
8. Pound's apartment
9. St. Luke's Chapel
10. Carrefour Vavin:
    Dôme
    Select
    Rotonde
11. The Dingo Bar (now Auberge du Centre)
12. Studio-Apartments Hôtel
13. Sign of the Black Manikin Press
14. Café Falstaff
15. Lavenue's
16. Café de Versailles
17. Hadley's apartment
18. Stein's apartment
19. Le Jardin du Luxembourg
20. Pelletier et Caventou statue

TOUR ONE

— Montparnasse ————————————————————

Nicknamed "Mount Parnassus" by Latin Quarter students who climbed here to recite poetry, Montparnasse became a center for Paris bohemians in the nineteenth century. By World War I, it had replaced Montmartre as the artistic center of the Parisian *avant garde.* Apollinaire, Max Jacobs, Lenin, Trotsky, Modigliani, and Picasso frequented its bars and cafés. Americans poured in during the twenties. Among them, of course, was Hemingway. This area is the richest in Hemingway associations in Paris. Much of *The Sun Also Rises* and *A Moveable Feast* is set here. The vast majority of places in this tour are cafés and restaurants.

You might wish to begin your walk from the Hôtel Beauvoir [13], a two-star hotel that Hadley stayed in in 1926 when she and Hemingway separated. You can best reach the Beauvoir by taking the Réseau Express Régional (RER) to Port Royal, the stop directly in front of the hotel. As you leave the station, turn to your left. The Beauvoir has a spectacular view of the Latin Quarter. From its sixth floor, you can see far to your right the trees of Le Jardin du Luxembourg, where Hemingway strolled, rising over the grey rooftops of Paris. Directly below you is the intersection of boulevards St. Michel and Montparnasse. The statue of Marshal Ney waves his sword at you where he stands before Hemingway's favorite café, La Closerie des Lilas. The narrow canyon to his right is Rue Notre-Dame-des-Champs, on which Hemingway and Ezra Pound lived. The broad length of the Boulevard du Montpar-

Hemingway and Hadley, 1922. *(Princeton University Library, Sylvia Beach Collection)*

nasse, the center of Left Bank life for American expatriates, lies to the left beneath you. In the distance rises the modern Tour du Montparnasse, whose glass monolith dominates the skyline.

As you leave the Beauvoir, to your right is an ugly modern building that stands on the site of the Bal Bullier [8], where Hemingway danced with his first two wives. Crossing the busy Boul' Mich' (student slang for the Boulevard St. Michel), we come to Marshal Ney's statue [83], Jake Barnes and Hemingway's confidant, which Rodin considered the best statue in Paris.

Behind him is La Closerie des Lilas [26]; here, Hemingway preferred *cafés crèmes*, which you can still get—large steaming cups of cream-laced coffee. The Hemingway connection is well-known here, and anyone can point out to you Hemingway's favorite bar stool. The *patron* speaks English; his mother, who may or may not be present, knew Papa. In fair weather, you should sit on La Closerie's terrace. Tree-shaded and removed from the street, it is one of the pleasantest terraces in Paris.

Leaving La Closerie, proceed down the Boulevard du Montparnasse. At the far end rises the modern Tour (Tower) Montparnasse, our destination and a good landmark if you wander off the beaten path. The tallest building in downtown Paris, it can be seen—to the dismay of many—from almost anywhere in the quarter.

The Boulevard du Montparnasse, the center of expatriate life in the Paris of the twenties, is lined with Hemingway sites. Sticking to the Closerie side of the street, we pass a pizzeria where, in Hemingway's day, stood Lavigne's Le Nègre de Toulouse [68]. The Nègre, a family restaurant, appears in both *The Sun Also Rises* and *A Moveable Feast*. Hemingway, Ford, Loeb, and others dined here, the Hemingways with such frequency that the owner, M. Lavigne, gave them their own napkins. Next door is the former Hôtel Venitia [126], where Hemingway trysted with Pauline.

A few doors down is a *boulangerie-patisserie* [19], which we must enter. This was Hemingway's shortcut to the Boulevard du Montparnasse from his apartment over the sawmill on Rue Notre-Dame-des-Champs. The current owner still lets *quartier* residents and Hemingway fans use her shop as a shortcut—and you should probably reward her generosity by picking up a croissant to munch on. Across from the *boulangerie*'s front door is the Rue Campagne Première. On this corner stood the original Jockey Club [62] (now at 127, Boulevard du Montparnasse). Popular with the expatriate crowd, it was Kiki's favorite club as well. Here, Hemingway danced with Josephine Baker, who was clad only in a floor-length black fur coat.

The *patisserie*'s back door lets out on Rue Notre-Dame-des-Champs. This narrow, quiet residential street is a stark contrast to the busy, broad Boulevard du Montparnasse you have just left. A look at the peeling facade of the *patisserie*'s rear wall takes you back to the Paris of the twenties. Unfortunately, the sawmill

Hemingway, Hadley, and Bumby lived above from 1924 to 1926 is gone. It stood across the street from the *patisserie*'s back door at 113 Rue Notre-Dame-des-Champs [53]. But its courtyard remains. You can enter this by the big gates at 117. The large paving blocks in the courtyard are those Hemingway, Pound, Fitzgerald, Dos Passos, and others trod.

Leaving the courtyard, turn right and proceed up Notre-Dame-des-Champs to the second left (Rue de Chevreuse). Were you to continue down Notre-Dame-des-Champs, you would come to 70 bis, where Ezra Pound lived [98]. On your right at 4, Rue de Chevreuse is Reid Hall, an American college student center. Here stood St. Luke's Chapel [109], where Bumby was christened in 1924 with Gertrude Stein as godmother. Ring the bell and enter. If you are permitted by the concierge, you can visit the quiet garden that runs to the next street, Rue de Chaumière. If you speak French, ask the concierge about La Maison Verte, a small green classroom building in the back with a tree growing out of its roof. She will tell you this is the actual chapel; the school's administration, however, thinks the chapel was torn down.

Leaving Reid Hall, continue up Chevreuse to Montparnasse. On the corner of Montparnasse and Chevreuse is today's Jockey Club [62]. Turning right, continue down the boulevard towards the Tour Montparnasse. The busy intersection ahead of you is the Carrefour Vavin, center of American expatriate life in the twenties. Its three cafés—the Rotonde (at 103), the Dôme (at 108), and the Select (at 99)—knew everyone who was anyone in literary Paris. Hemingway and Hadley warmed themselves with rum punches at the Dôme [33] at Christmas in 1923. Look up at the building's roof line to see how it earned its name. Hemingway damned the rival Rotonde [106] as a backwater for Greenwich Village scum, although its art gallery was legendary, and other Americans— including Sinclair Lewis—knew it. Next door to the Rotonde is the Select [111], favorite bar of horse-race wizard Harold Stearns, who furnished the prototype for *The Sun Also Rises*' Harvey Stone. Here Frances Clyne insulted her two-timing lover, Robert Cohn, while Jake Barnes snuck out through the corner door onto Rue Vavin; we shall, too.

Across the street we pass by the Dôme, whose seafood dinners rated a *toque* (chef's hat—a mark of excellence) in Paris restaurant guides and may tempt you back this evening. Behind the Dôme is

Rue Delambre. On the Dôme side several doors down at number 10 is the Auberge du Centre, a well-known restaurant of good food and fair prices. Its friendly chef has photos of it from Hemingway's day. The exterior and interior are much the same as they were when Jimmy "the Barman" Charters ran the Dingo bar [32] here. It was at the Dingo bar—still standing—that Hemingway first met Fitzgerald. Present also were Lady Duff Twysden and Pat Guthrie, the models for Brett Ashley and Mike Campbell of *The Sun Also Rises*. Across the street still stands the Studio-Apartments Hôtel [117], Twysden's residence in 1925, and the probable model for Ashley's hotel in *The Sun Also Rises*.

Heading back to Montparnasse we glance at number 4, Rue Delambre. Here Edward Titus had his bookstore and Sign of the Black Manikin Press [113], which published in 1930 Kiki's memoirs, to which Hemingway wrote an introduction—his first.

Back on the Boulevard du Montparnasse, we turn left and continue approaching the Tour Montparnasse. We pass by the Coupole, which Hemingway probably knew, but failed to mention. Its interior dates from the twenties and is worth a look. When you reach the first street corner—Rue du Montparnasse—remark the Falstaff's white neon sign. Half a block down on the left at number 42, the Café Falstaff [36] was where bartender Charters moved when he left the Dingo. The Falstaff is still a bar and restaurant with an authentic interior. It was probably on the sidewalk here that Hemingway decked McAlmon in 1929 for spreading rumors that Hemingway was gay.

Continuing down the boulevard, we come to the Place du 18 Juin 1940. The Tour is now in full view. Imagine, however, a large square and train station, for so it was when Hemingway knew it. Should you have been unable to enter the Beauvoir, you might cross the street to the Galleries Lafeyette, a chain department store. From their terrace, you can get a free view of the nearby quarter. On the corner, at 68–70 Boulevard du Montparnasse, is a brasserie. Above its wooden facade you can see cut in stone "Lavenue" [67]. This was the famous hotel and restaurant Lavenue's that Jake Barnes, Robert Cohn, and Frances Clyne dined at in the first chapter of *The Sun Also Rises*. Hemingway, Loeb, and Cannell dined here in real life too.

Cross now to the other side of the Boulevard and follow the sidewalk as it curves to the right towards the Rue de Rennes. Chez

Hansi's brasserie stands where the Café de Versailles [127] stood in the twenties. An after-hours café, the Versailles saw Barnes and Cohn as well. You, too, can visit it after hours, as it stays open to the wee hours of the morning.

Descend Rue de Rennes towards the Seine, putting the Tour du Montparnasse at your back. This is a longish block devoid of Hemingway sites. But the first street to your right that you come to is the Rue de Notre-Dame-des-Champs, whose other end you visited earlier on this tour. Turn right (there is a good bakery here if you are hungry) and then take the first left. You should be at the Rue de Fleurus. Cross the Boulevard Raspail and continue on Fleurus. To your right you will find 35 and 27. The first (demolished in 1988) is where Hadley moved with Bumby in 1926 after Hemingway deserted her for Pauline [55]. Number 27 was Gertrude Stein's famous studio [116]. Stein's apartment became a center of the American expatriate group. A plaque on the wall giving her name is one of the very few you will find for any of this group in Paris. Hemingway and Hadley visited Stein

Alice B. Toklas and Gertrude Stein with infant Bumby, 1924.
(Courtesy Ernest Hemingway Collection, John F. Kennedy Library)

regularly at first, and Stein claims it was she to whom he came for advice when Hadley informed him she was pregnant. Here, too, he claims he heard Stein and Alice B. Toklas in the lovers' quarrel that marked the end of Hemingway's tutelage.

Continue down Rue de Fleurus until it dead-ends at Le Jardin du Luxembourg [59]. A welcome respite from the concrete of Paris, the Luxembourg was a Hemingway favorite. If it is summer, you can watch the children of Paris sailing their boats in the lake much as Thomas Hudson watched his son do in *Islands in the Stream*. The palace to your left is the Palais du Luxembourg, the French Senate. To its left as you face it is the former Musée du Luxembourg, where a hungry Hemingway went to study Cezanne instead of eating. The paintings are now in the Musée D'Orsay.

On the other side of the lake is the ornate Fountain des Médicis. Here Hemingway is said to have killed pigeons to eat. You can buy peanuts from vendors outside the park to feed the pigeons and try your luck at wringing their necks.

After resting your feet for a while on one of the many benches in the park, you will have to decide how tired you are. You can, if you are feeling energetic, supplement this tour with either Tour Two or Three, both of which pass through the Luxembourg.

If, however, you are tired, stand with the palace to your back. To your right you should see the Tour Montparnasse rising above the Paris skyline. Proceed straight through the park. At the Rue Auguste Comte you can take a short, one-block detour to the left to the Boulevard St. Michel. Across the street you will see a statue of a reclining woman [87]. This replaces the statue to the inventors of pharmacy that Jake Barnes and Bill Gorton notice on their drunken stroll through Paris. Here you can take a right and continue back up Boulevard St. Michel to the Beauvoir. Or you may return to the park, and take a left. This tree-lined extension of the Luxembourg Gardens will take you back to the Closerie des Lilas where we began. It was by this route that Hemingway would leave the sawmill apartment on the Rue Notre-Dame-des-Champs (which will appear to your right as you leave the park) and descend to the Luxembourg.

We are now back at the Closerie, where you should stop for a bourbon, Hemingway's *boisson préférée*, according to the owners.

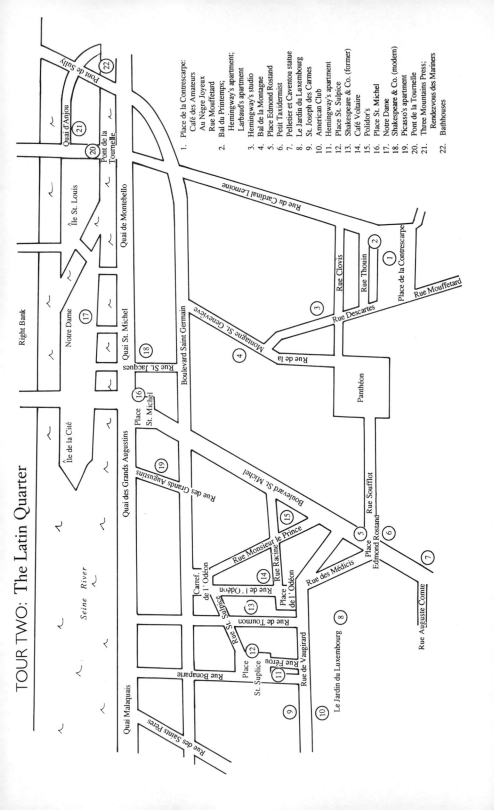

TOUR TWO: The Latin Quarter

1. Place de la Contrescarpe:
   Café des Amateurs
   Au Nègre Joyeux
   Rue Mouffetard
2. Bal du Printemps;
   Hemingway's apartment;
   Larbaud's apartment
3. Hemingway's studio
4. Bal de la Montagne
5. Place Edmond Rostand
6. Petit Taxidermist
7. Pelletier et Caventou statue
8. Le Jardin du Luxembourg
9. St. Joseph des Carmes
10. American Club
11. Hemingway's apartment
12. Place St. Sulpice
13. Shakespeare & Co. (former)
14. Café Voltaire
15. Polidor's
16. Place St. Michel
17. Notre Dame
18. Shakespeare & Co. (modern)
19. Picasso's apartment
20. Pont de la Tournelle
21. Three Mountains Press;
    Rendezvous des Mariners
22. Bathhouses

TOUR TWO
— The Latin Quarter ————————————————

The Latin Quarter's student flavor began in the twelfth century when students, clerks, and teachers escaped here from the Île de la Cité and its bishops. The Sorbonne remains one of world's most renowned universities, though today it shares Paris's 200,000 students with over ten other universities. With the Jardin du Luxembourg separating it from the Montparnasse district, this area was, for the expatriates, relatively quiet. Many of the sites here are residential or business.

We begin at the Place de la Contrescarpe [91], whose closest Métro stop is Monge. This seedy square is about as close to *la France profonde* as you will get in this area of Paris. Even in Hemingway's day, the Latin Quarter was becoming middle class. On the fringes of the Quarter proper, the Place de la Contrescarpe is only now being renovated. Enjoy it while it lasts.

La Chope at numbers 2 and 4 was formerly the Café des Amateurs [1] that Hemingway avoided in *A Moveable Feast*. But its clientele today are not nearly as rummy as they were in his day, and you should start your tour by enjoying a coffee on its terrace. If it is warm, you will probably see several *clochards* lounging with their dogs in the sun in the square. To your right, over the gaudy yellow facade of the Codec grocery store, is a sign to Au Nègre Joyeux [81], sole remnant of the bar Jake Barnes bypassed in *The Sun Also Rises*. To your left, over the storefronts, you can read in the stone "Maison de la Pomme de Pin MCC," purportedly the site of Rabelais' tavern of the same name. The narrow Rue Mouffetard slopes from Place de la Contrescarpe to the Avenue des Gobelins. Walk it if you have time; both Hemingway and Henry Miller loved it.

After you finish your coffee, you should turn left and walk down the Rue du Cardinal Lemoine. Immediately to your left you will find 74. Here is Le Rayon Vert Disco, today's version of Hemingway's Bal du Printemps [10]. Its garish green and black exterior suggests it harbors a clientele little improved since Hemingway's day. Next to it is an herbalist's run by Simone, who claims she knew Hemingway. She and he used to sit on the stoop and trade tales, she says.

Should luck be with you, you will find the door to 74 open and you can climb the stairs to Hemingway's third-floor apartment [52]. The toilets he remembered in *A Moveable Feast* are still on each landing, although their doors are locked.

Across the street a few doors down, number 71 Cardinal Lemoine housed James Joyce the year before Hemingway arrived in Paris. Valery Larbaud [66] had lent it to him. Hemingway and Hadley knew Larbaud, and probably visited him here.

Take a left at Rue Thouin. A short block will bring you out on Rue Descartes. A block and a half to your right, sandwiched between two quaint restaurants, number 39 was where Hemingway rented a room to write during his first year in Paris [50]. A plaque marks the building as that where Verlaine died.

Follow Rue Descartes to where it meets the narrow Rue de la Montagne Ste. Geneviève. At 46 Ste. Geneviève stood a gay *bal musette*, model for one in *The Sun Also Rises* where we first meet Brett [9]. Turn left and climb the Rue de la Montagne Ste. Geneviève to the Panthéon.

Leaving the Panthéon, proceed two blocks down Rue Soufflot to the Place Edmond Rostand [92], across from the Luxembourg Gardens. On the corner of Soufflot and the Boulevard St. Michel, you can stop at the Free Time Hamburger. In the twenties, this was the Luxembourg Café, where Hemingway and Jake Barnes ate breakfast before catching the bus to the Right Bank. Across Soufflot is McDonald's, should you be homesick. Should you still like France, you might prefer the more typically French Luxembourg Bar across the Boulevard St. Michel.

Half a block up the Boulevard St. Michel to your left is number

81. A plaque tells you a German bomb dropped here during World War I. During the twenties, it housed a taxidermist, and Jake and Bill stop here on their drunken stroll through Paris to admire its stuffed animals [89]. A little farther up is a new monument to Pelletier and Caventou, discoverers of quinine; Barnes and Gorton stumbled by the previous statue at this site [87].

Returning to Place Edmond Rostand, you can cross to the Jardin du Luxembourg [59]. Before entering, buy some peanuts from the vendor who stands near the gate. Once inside, look for the large fountain on your right. This, the Fontain des Médicis, was where a hungry Hemingway is said to have bagged pigeons for Hadley's oven. You might wish to try the same before walking over to admire the lake where Bumby sailed his boats. Gertrude Stein walked her dog along these tree-lined allées. To the left of the Luxembourg Palace, which houses the French Senate, was the Musée Luxembourg. Here Hemingway learned composition from Cezanne and rendezvoused with Pauline while Hadley was out of town.

(At this point you may switch to either Tour One or Tour Three; both pass through the Luxembourg. Tour One will lead you towards Montparnasse, Tour Three towards the Right Bank.)

Leave the Luxembourg by the exit on Rue de Vaugirard next to the museum. Across the street and a block and a half to the left at 70, Rue de Vaugirard is the baroque church St. Joseph des Carmes [108]. Here an impotent Hemingway came to pray at Pauline's request. His prayers answered, Hemingway converted to Catholicism.

Across the street from St. Joseph's is 33, Rue de Vaugirard. Today a cafeteria, in 1929 it probably housed the American Club [2]. Here Morley Callaghan decked Hemingway while Scott Fitzgerald kept the clock. Callaghan chronicles the ensuing contretemps in *That Summer in Paris.*

Returning to the Musée Luxembourg, you should look for Rue Férou on your left. Halfway down this quiet street, whose pavées the French have not yet taken up, is number 6. Guarded by crouching sphinxes, this courtyard leads to the seven-room apartment Hemingway shared with Pauline after he left Hadley [54]. Thinking back to Cardinal Lemoine's scaling facade and seedy *quartier* will provide a good measure of how high Hemingway climbed the social ladder by marrying Pauline.

Férou dead-ends in the Place St. Sulpice. Newly converted Hemingway and devout Pauline attended mass here at St. Sulpice [110] Sundays before taking in the races. In *A Moveable Feast,* Hemingway remembers the fountain in the center and the religious stores around the square.

Leaving the square to the left of the church, you find yourself on the Rue St. Sulpice. Pass Rue de Tournon and turn right at Rue de l'Odéon. On your right you will pass number 12. Sylvia Beach's Shakespeare and Company stood here until World War II forced her to close [112]. Hemingway borrowed books from her library, used this as a mailing address, and gave one of his rare public readings here to help her out during the Great Depression.

Beach lived with her lover Adrienne Monnier at number 18 [12]. Hemingway liberated them in August, 1944, killing the German sniper on their roof and taking their last bar of soap. Monnier ran La Maison des Amis des Livres at number 7, the French

James Joyce and Sylvia Beach in Shakespeare and Company, 1920. *(Princeton University Library, Sylvia Beach Collection)*

equivalent of and model for Beach's bookstore. Both stores are gone, but the bookstore at number 10 has the same floor plan as did Beach's—as the owner will tell you should you ask. Number 8 briefly housed Robert McAlmon's Contact Editions, which published Hemingway's first book, *Three Stories and Ten Poems*.

Rue de l'Odéon dead-ends at the Place de l'Odéon. The theatre before you is le Théâtre National de l'Odéon. Number 1 houses a Franco-American organization, should you need a translator. In Hemingway's day this was the Café-Restaurant Voltaire [130], once frequented by the eighteenth-century Encyclopedists and later by French literati. Here Hemingway and Allen Tate fell out over just how indebted to Defoe Hemingway was.

By now, you are probably ready for a break and a bite to eat. Take the Rue Racine to your left as you look at the theatre. A short block away you will come upon Rue Monsieur le Prince, whose name recalls the patronym for the king's brother. Two doors from the corner is Polidor's Crémerie and Restaurant [94]. Unmentioned by Hemingway, Polidor's fed him, according to its former owner. The interior remains unchanged from Hemingway's day, and the menu was, at last visit, traditional and moderate. You can get Cahors here, Hemingway's *vin préférée*. And the apple pie with cream will put mother's to shame.

After lunch, if you are not ready to go back to your hotel, you might continue along Rue Racine to its intersection with the Boulevard St. Michel. To your right, a block up, is the Sorbonne, whose young students Jake Barnes and Hemingway admired as they passed the Luxembourg Café a block farther up.

The Boul' Mich' runs down to the Seine, and we shall follow it.

At the foot of the Boulevard St. Michel, today's Place St. Michel is far too busy to harbor writers at work. But it was in a café here that Hemingway wrote short stories in quieter days [93]. Along the Seine are the bookstalls of Paris [18], which Hemingway frequented in his search for second-hand American books. You can cross the river to the Île de la Cité and climb Notre Dame's tower if you want a close-up of the gargoyles scowling towards Germany that Hemingway told his *Star* readers about [20]. Or you can detour several blocks out of your way to the Rue des Grands Augustins, a quaint old street where Picasso lived at number 7 [90].

Back on the Left Bank, you should stroll along the quais upriver towards the Île St. Louis. Across from Notre Dame, on the corner of Rue St. Jacques and Quai St. Michel, is the modern-day Shakespeare and Company [112]. Its red and green facade is much quainter than the one Hemingway knew, but the store, a mecca for American students, is worth visiting; ask to see the Sylvia Beach Memorial Room. Farther up the Seine you reach the Pont de la Tournelle [96], which is where Jake and Bill cross in *The Sun Also Rises*. The view downriver towards Notre Dame is that of a thousand postcards. With luck, you will be standing here while a *bateau mouche* slides under the bridge. These barges, Hemingway told his *Star* readers, drew Parisians looking for cheap alternatives to Parisian apartments. Moored at a *quai*, the barges could—and still do—provide relatively cheap lodging. From time to time, an ad for one appears on the blackboard outside today's Shakespeare and Company. The next bridge upriver is the Pont de Sully [95]. Next to it stood the public, cold-water bathhouse the Hemingways used in the twenties.

View from the Pont de la Tournelle: a *bateau mouche* with Notre Dame in the background.

Once across the Pont de la Tournelle, you are on the Île St. Louis. Cross the island by taking the Rue des Deux Ponts to the Quai d'Anjou, which begins on your right. Several doors down are numbers 29 and 33. Number 29 housed Ford Madox Ford's *transatlantic review*, for which Hemingway worked. Here too was Bill Bird's Three Mountains Press [120], which published Hemingway's *in our time*. Here Hemingway met Harold Loeb for the first time, whom he would later savage as Robert Cohn in *The Sun Also Rises*. At 33 was Madame Lecomte's Au Rendezvous des Mariners, where Hemingway and Jake Barnes dined until the American Women's Club invaded it [103].

If you continue along the Quai d'Anjou to its end at the Pont de Sully, you will find a quiet backwater. Often choked with grass where ducks feed in the spring and summer, this a favorite Parisian fishing spot. With luck, you will find someone fishing here, using much the same equipment that Hemingway described in *A Moveable Feast*.

TOUR THREE: Both Banks at Once

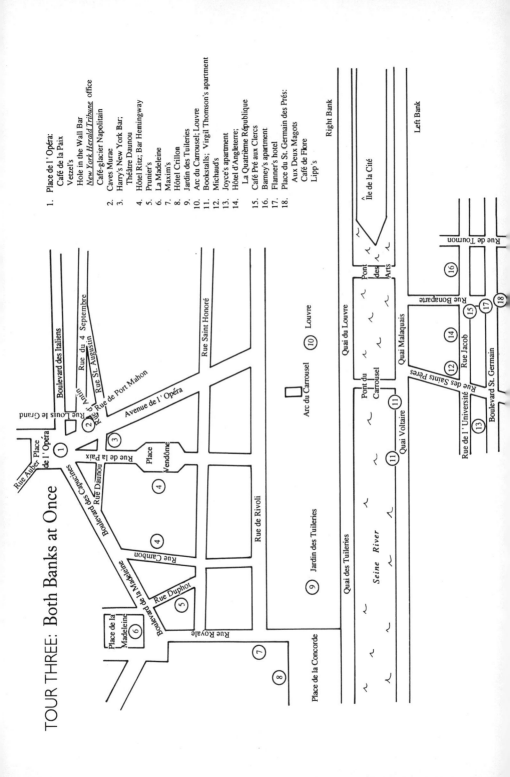

1. Place de l'Opéra:
   Café de la Paix
   Vetzel's
   Hole in the Wall Bar
   New York Herald Tribune office
   Café-glacier Napolitain
2. Caves Murae
3. Harry's New York Bar;
   Théâtre Daunou
4. Hôtel Ritz; Bar Hemingway
5. Prunier's
6. La Madeleine
7. Maxim's
8. Hôtel Crillon
9. Jardin des Tuileries
10. Arc du Carrousel; Louvre
11. Bookstalls; Virgil Thomson's apartment
12. Michaud's
13. Joyce's apartment
14. Hôtel d'Angleterre;
    La Quatrième République
15. Café Pré aux Clercs
16. Barney's apartment
17. Flanner's hotel
18. Place du St. Germain des Prés:
    Aux Deux Magots
    Café de Flore
    Lipp's

TOUR THREE

— Both Banks at Once ───────────

This tour spans both sides of the Seine. On the Right Bank, it takes in some of the classiest restaurants and hotels in Paris, whose Hemingway connections date mostly from after he achieved fame and fortune. A number, however, are associated with his early newspaper days. Crossing the river to the Left Bank, we enter the early Hemingway years. Here we pass by a number of residential sites and visit some of Paris's most famous cafés.

Begin at the Place de l'Opéra. The Café de la Paix [84], on your left as you look at the Opéra, drew Hemingway and Hadley their first Christmas in Paris. New to town and French money, they overspent and Hadley remained as hostage while Hemingway ran across the river and back in search of money. You'd better have money too, because the Paix is expensive—though its terrace view of honking cars hardly seems worth the price. The Paix's entrance on Rue Auber stands where Vetzel's Brasserie stood in *The Sun Also Rises* when Jake and Cohn stopped by [128].

Across from the Paix at 23, Boulevard des Capucines is the Hole in the Wall Bar [58]. Today a Spanish bar and restaurant, in Hemingway's day it was a den for dope dealers. Here Ezra Pound bought opium, according to *A Moveable Feast*.

Behind you as you face the Opéra is the Rue de la Paix. Number 49 housed the *New York Herald Tribune*'s office in Hemingway's day [82]. There were a number of newspaper offices in the area;

Ezra Pound in Shakespeare and Company, early
1920s. *(Photo by Sylvia Beach, Princeton University
Library, Sylvia Beach Collection)*

today they have all moved, and the bars and cafés that catered to
newsmen have for the most part changed hands and character.

To your right as you face the Opéra is the Boulevard des
Capucines. The Hippopotame Restaurant—a chain steak house—
at number 51 replaces Jake Barnes's Café-glacier Napolitain [80].
Here Jake picked up the *poule* Georgette; today's *poules* have moved
a ways off the boulevard. You can still find them, though they

seem to walk less than in Jake's day, preferring to stand in the doorways leading to their rooms.

Leaving the Hippopotame, take a right down the Rue Louis le Grand. Continue along this street until you reach the first intersection. You will be at the Rue du 4 Septembre. Cross over and look for a small street cutting off to the left. This is the Rue de Port Mahon. A block down on your right, turn into the Rue d'Antin. You will find halfway down the block at number 19 on your right the café Aux Cloches de VilleDieu. This is an undiscovered French bar which stands where the Caves Murae stood in Hemingway's day [21]. The Caves had the best and cheapest booze in town, Hemingway wrote Loeb. Aux Cloches may not be the cheapest, but it is authentic. And its bartender will tell you, if you speak French, that it was a favorite of Jacques Brel.

Rue d'Antin intersects the Avenue de l'Opéra. Across the street is Rue Daunou. A few doors up on your left is Harry's New York Bar [49]. Enter it; order a drink. Harry's was—and is—an expatriate hangout *par excellence*. Its interior, unchanged since the twenties, recalls deliberately a pre-Prohibition American college bar. A few doors beyond is the Théâtre Daunou, whose club if not theatre Hemingway knew [30].

Rue Daunou crosses the Rue de la Paix. Turning left on this street, you will see the Column Vendôme rising before you. Follow it to the Place Vendôme, where the Hôtel Ritz is on your right [104]. This, the original "ritzy" place, became Papa Hemingway's favorite Parisian hotel. Here he left in 1927 the notebooks which would become *A Moveable Feast* when he rediscovered them in the fifties. Hemingway and his band of *maquis* liberated the Ritz in 1944, earning as their reward martinis on the house.

If you have money, you can even stay in one of Hemingway's rooms. Or eat in the Ritz's restaurant, which has named a plate after Papa. Poorer aficionados might simply take the short cut through the Ritz to the back door on Rue Cambon. There, to your left as you leave the hotel, to your right as you enter, is the Bar Hemingway. This was Papa's (and Fitzgerald's) favorite Ritz bar. Hemingway memorabilia line the walls; a bust stands on the bar, and the French barman is friendly and willing to talk.

Leave the Ritz by the Rue Cambon and turn left. At the end of the block, turn right up the Rue Duphot. On your left you will see Prunier's [100]. A celebrated seafood restaurant, Prunier's fed

Hemingway and Hadley when they had luck at the races. After he became rich, Papa ate here with the likes of Marlene Dietrich. The interior is original, and the seafood excellent but costly.

Rue Duphot ends at the Place de la Madeleine. Hemingway witnessed Big Bertha's bomb burst against the back of La Madeleine [75] in 1918.

From the front steps of La Madeleine, you can look down the Rue Royale to the Place de la Concorde. Maxim's is at number 3. A rich Papa perhaps appreciated this renowned restaurant, but it gave a poorer and younger Hemingway a headache [76]. It was at the Hôtel Crillon's bar at 10, Place de la Concorde that Hemingway drank when he worked for the newspapers [28]. Jake Barnes also drank here while waiting for Brett in *The Sun Also Rises*. Their bar is gone, but you can still drink here.

Leaving the Crillon, you will find the Jardin des Tuileries [61] to your left. Hemingway reserved this garden for his lovers. In *The Sun Also Rises*, Jake and Georgette ride through the park. In *A Moveable Feast*, Hemingway and Hadley stroll here. If you cut through the garden until you pass through the Arc du Carrousel, you will be standing where they stood. You should do this at night, as they did. Then you can—ignoring the traffic and streetlamps—enjoy the view through the Carrousel to the Champs-Elysées and the Arc du Triomphe beyond. In *A Moveable Feast* he and Hadley wonder if these two arches are, as they have heard, on a line with the Sermione in Milan. On the map, they appear to be.

Across from the Carrousel is the entrance to the Louvre. You might wish to examine the male statues here. This is what Hemingway advised Fitzgerald to do in *A Moveable Feast*. Crossing the Seine by the Pont du Carrousel, you will be on the rive gauche, with the Quai Voltaire to your right. Here are the bookstalls [18] that Hemingway frequented. Number 17 Quai Voltaire was American composer Virgil Thomson's apartment for a number of years [119]. Thomson, a friend of Stein's, collaborated with Hemingway on his film, *The Spanish Earth*. But he disliked the hard-drinking Hemingway, whom he associated with the expatriate crowd of Montparnasse.

The Rue des Saints Pères lies just ahead, on the left. Walking up this street you will be following the trace of Hemingway and Hadley on their way home from Prunier's one evening. You, too, may be hungry by the time you reach the corner of Rue Jacob. If so, stop at L'Escorailles. This café stands where Michaud's restaurant stood in the twenties [77]. Hemingway and Hadley ate here, and Hemingway examined Fitzgerald's natural endowments in the bathroom and pronounced them adequate. The bathroom has been remodeled, but it contains a typical WC *turc*—Hemingway's "squat toilet"—if you have not encountered one. L'Escorailles' waiters know more about Michaud than they do Hemingway or Fitzgerald. But if enough people stop by, they will no doubt learn quickly.

Leaving L'Escorailles, a short walk to your right up Rue de l'Université will bring you to number 9, where James Joyce was living in 1922 when Hemingway first met him [63]. Returning to L'Escorailles, you will be on Rue Jacob, a street rich with Hemingway associations. The three-star Hôtel d'Angleterre at 44 Rue Jacob housed Hemingway and Hadley upon their arrival in Paris in 1921 [6]. You could have their room, number 14, for only 690 francs a night in 1987. Next door at 42 was the La Quatrième République, whose Christmas dinner Hemingway panned in a newspaper article [101]. Il Casanova serves Italian food here today. At the corner of Rues Jacob and Bonaparte is the Café Pré aux Clercs [99]. Here Hemingway dined for 12 francs; you can get a coffee for nearly the same price. Natalie Barney lived farther down Jacob at number 20. Enter through the wooden portal if you want to see the two-story *pavillon* at the end of the courtyard where she entertained Hemingway, Pound, and others at her literary salon [11].

If you backtrack and turn left on Rue Bonaparte, you will pass the Hôtel St. Germain des Prés at number 36. Here Hemingway used to visit Janet Flanner, who was *The New Yorker*'s Paris correspondent [39].

Rue Bonaparte ends at the Place St. Germain des Prés. This square is flanked on one side by Paris's oldest church, St. Germain des Prés, on the other by one of her most famous cafés, Aux Deux Magots [31]. One of Les Trois Grandes, the French equivalent of the American center at the Carrefour Vavin, the Deux Magots became a Hemingway hangout after *The Sun Also Rises* poisoned his relations with the expatriates. With the Café de Flore at 172, Boulevard St. Germain [41] and Lipp's [70] across the street at 151, Aux Deux Magots gave Hemingway a new group of friends. Among these was James Joyce, with whom Hemingway drank to the chagrin of Joyce's wife Nora. As Hemingway befriended Joyce, he had to ignore Stein. The two were rivals with little use for each other. Hemingway remained friends with Joyce; he fell out with Stein.

Lipp's bright orange awning makes it easy to spot. Here Hemingway is said to have sat awaiting Harold Loeb, the model for *The Sun Also Rises'* Robert Cohn. According to Charters, Loeb was one of six characters in search of the author—with a gun. They never shot him, though. Lipp's *cervalas remoulade* and draft beer filled a hungry Hemingway in the twenties. Paris guidebooks give both food and drink rave reviews today.

The Flore became a Hemingway writing café. Today it is as popular with foreigners as with natives. For a while after World War II, the Flore was a celebrated gay bar.

Place St. Germain des Prés is only two blocks away from Place St. Sulpice (see Map Two). If you continue down Rue Bonaparte away from the river, you can link up with Tour Two.

— BIBLIOGRAPHY

Acheson, Edward C. *Password to Paris*. New York: William
  Morrow & Co., 1932.
Baedeker, Karl. *Paris and Environs*. Leipzig: Karl Baedeker, 1913.
———. *Paris and Environs*. Leipzig: Karl Baedeker, 1924.
Baker, Carlos. *Ernest Hemingway: A Life Story*. New York:
  Scribner's, 1969.
———. *Hemingway and his Critics*. New York: Hill & Wang,
  1961.
Bayard, Jean-Emile. *Le quartier latin, hier et aujourd'hui*. Paris:
  Jouve, 1924.
Beach, Sylvia. *Shakespeare and Company*. New York: Harcourt,
  Brace, 1951.
The Blue Guides. Paris and Environs. Edited by Ian Robertson.
  London: Ernest Benn Limited, 1977.
Bournon, Fernand. *La Voie Publique et son Decor*, in *Les Richesses
  d'Art de la Ville de Paris*. Paris: H. Laurens, 1909.
Boyle, Kay. *See* McAlmon, Robert.
Brassai (pseudonymn for Gyula Halasz). *The Secret Paris of the
  Thirties*. Translated by Richard Miller. N.Y.: Pantheon Books,
  1976.
Bruccoli, Matthew J. and Duggan, Margaret M. Duggan, eds.
  Correspondence of F. Scott Fitzgerald. New York: Random
  House, 1980.
Brumback, Theodore. Article, title missing, in *Kansas City Star*,
  Dec. 6, 1936.
Burnand, Robert. *Le guide du gourmand à Paris*. Paris: B. Grasset,
  1925.

Callaghan, Morley. *That Summer in Paris*. New York: Penguin Books, 1963.

Charters, James. *This Must Be the Place: Memoirs of Montparnasse*. Edited by Morrill Cody. London: H. Joseph Ltd., 1934.

Collins, Larry and Lapierre, Dominique. *Is Paris Burning?* New York: Pocket Books, 1977.

Coussillan, Jacques. *Dictionnaire historique des Rues de Paris*. Paris: Editions de minuit, 1963.

Crosby, Caresse. *The Passionate Years*. London: Alvin Redman, 1955.

Crosby, Harry. *Shadows of the Sun*. Edited by Edward Germain. Santa Barbara, Calif.: Black Sparrow Press, 1977.

Didot-Bottin. *Almanache du commerce de Paris*. Paris, 1920–1930.

Dos Passos, John. *The Best Times: An Informal Memoir*. New York: New American Library, 1966.

Elliot, Paul. *The Last Time I Saw Paris*. New York: Random House, 1942.

Ellmann, Richard. *James Joyce*. New York: Oxford University Press, 1959.

Fitch, Noel Riley. *Sylvia Beach and the Lost Generation*. New York: Norton, 1983.

Flanner, Janet. *An American in Paris*. New York: Simon & Schuster, 1940.

————. *Paris Journals*. 2 vols. Edited by William Shawn. New York: Atheneum, 1965.

————. *Paris Was Yesterday*. Edited by Irving Drutman. New York: Viking Press, 1972.

Ford, Ford Madox. *It Was the Nightingale*. London: William Heinemann Ltd., 1934.

Fuss-Amoré, Gustave and Ombiaux, Maurice des. *Montparnasse*. Paris: Albin Michel, 1925.

Gajdusek, Robert E. *Hemingway's Paris*. New York: Scribner's, 1978.

Le Gallienne, Richard. *From a Paris Garret*. New York: I. Washburn, 1936.

————. *From a Paris Scrapbook*. New York: I. Washburn, 1938.

Gault, Henri and Millau, Christian. *A Parisian's Guide to Paris*. New York: Random House, 1969.

————. *Guide Julliard de Paris*. Paris: Julliard, 1965.

Gilot, Francoise and Lake, Carlton. *Life with Picasso*. New York: McGraw Hill, 1964.

Griffin, Peter. *Along With Youth: Hemingway, the Early Years*. New York: Oxford University Press, 1985.

Guide Littéraire de la France. Bibliothèque des Guides Bleus. Paris: Libraire Hachette, 1964.

Hawkins, Eric. *Hawkins of the Paris Herald*. New York: Simon & Schuster, 1963.

Hemingway, Ernest. *Across the River and Into the Trees*. New York: Scribner's, 1950.

———. *Byline: Ernest Hemingway*. Edited by William White. New York: Scribner's, 1967.

———. *Dateline: Toronto*. Edited by William White. New York: Scribner's, 1985.

———. *A Farewell To Arms*. New York: Scribner's, 1930.

———. *The First Forty-Nine Stories*. London: Jonathan Cape, 1962.

———. *For Whom the Bell Tolls*. New York: Scribner's, 1940 .

———. *The Garden of Eden*. New York: Scribner's, 1986.

———. *Green Hills of Africa*. Garden City, N.Y.: Permabooks, 1954.

———. "How We Came to Paris," *Collier's*, vol. 114, no. 15 (October, 7, 1944).

———. *Islands in the Stream*. New York: Scribner's, 1970.

———. *A Moveable Feast*. New York: Scribner's, 1964.

———. *Selected Letters 1917–1961*. Edited by Carlos Baker. New York: Scribner's, 1981.

———. *The Sun Also Rises*. New York: Scribner's, 1970.

———. *Three Stories and Ten Poems*. Paris: Contact Pub. Co., 1923; reprinted 1977.

———. *Torrents of Spring*. New York: Scribner's, 1926.

Hemingway, Mary Walsh. *How It Was*. New York: Alfred A. Knopf, 1976.

Hotchner, A. E. *Papa Hemingway*. New York: Random House, 1966.

Huddleston, Sisley. *Back to Montparnasse*. New York: J. B. Lippincott Company, 1931.

Huisman, Georges and Poisson, Georges. *Les Monuments de Paris*. Paris: Librairie Hachette, 1966.

Joyce, James. *Letters of James Joyce*. Edited by Richard Ellmann. New York: Viking Press, 1966.

Kent, Bernice. *The Hemingway Women*. New York: W. W. Norton & Company, 1983.

Kiki. *Memoires*. Translated by Samuel Putnam. Seven Sirens Press, 1955.

Kiley, Jed. *Hemingway: An Old Friend Remembers*. New York: Hawthorn Books, 1965.

Laney, Al. *Paris Herald*. New York: D. Appleton-Century Company, 1947.

Lewis, Sinclair. "Self-Conscious America," in *The American Mercury*, vol. 6, no. 22 (Oct., 1926).

Loeb, Harold. *The Way It Was*. New York: Criterion Books, 1959.

Lynn, Kenneth S. *Hemingway*. New York: Simon & Schuster, 1987.

MacLeish, Archibald. *A Continuing Journey*. Boston: Houghton Mifflin, 1968.

————. *Letters of Archibald MacLeish*. Edited by R. H. Winnick. Boston: Houghton Mifflin, 1983.

Mayfield, Sara. *Exiles from Paradise*. New York: Delacorte Press, 1971.

McAlmon, Robert. *Being Geniuses Together 1920–1930*. Revised and with supplementary chapters by Kay Boyle. Garden City, N.Y.: Doubleday, 1968.

McMillan, Dougald. *transition: The History of a Literary Era 1927–1938*. New York: George Braziller, 1975.

Mellow, James R. *Charmed Circle: Gertrude Stein and Company*. New York: Praeger Publishers, 1974.

————. *Invented Lives: F. Scott and Zelda Fitzgerald*. Boston: Houghton Mifflin, 1984.

Meyer, Jeffrey. *Hemingway: A Biography*. New York: Harper & Row, 1985.

Michelin. *Paris: Guide de Tourisme*. 4th ed. Paris: Pneu Michelin.

Miller, Henry W. *The Paris Gun*. New York: Jonathan Cape and Harrison Smith, 1930.

Morton, Brian N. *Americans in Paris*. Ann Arbor, Mich.: The Olivia and Hill Press, 1984.

Muirhead's Paris and its Environs. The Blue Guides. Edited by
Findlay Muirhead and Marcel Monmarche. London:
Macmillan, 1927.
Orgrizek, Dore. *The Paris We Love.* New York: McGraw Hill,
1950.
————. *France, Paris and the Provinces.* Translated by Margeurite
Bigot and Madeline Blaess. New York: Whittlesey House,
1948.
Putnam, Samuel. *Paris Was Our Mistress.* New York: Viking
Press, 1947.
Reynolds, Bruce. *Paris With the Lid Lifted.* New York: George
Sully and Company, 1927.
Robert, Robert. *See* Burnand, Robert.
Root, Waverley. *The Paris Edition: The Autobiography of Waverley
Root, 1927–1934.* Edited by Samuel Abt. San Francisco:
North Point Press, 1987.
Sarason, Bertram. *Hemingway and the "Sun" Set.* Washington,
D. C.: NCR Microcard Editions, 1972.
Simon, Kate. *Paris places and pleasures; an uncommon guidebook.*
New York: G. P. Putnam's Sons, 1967.
Slocombe, George. *Paris in Profile.* Boston: Houghton Mifflin,
1929.
Smith, Frank B. *The Real Latin Quarter.* New York: Funk &
Wagnalls, 1901.
Sokoloff, Alice Hunt. *Hadley: The First Mrs. Hemingway.* New
York: Dodd, Mead & Company, 1973.
Stearns, Harold. *Confessions of a Harvard Man.* Edited by Hugh
Ford. Sutton West and Santa Barbara, Calif.: Paget Press,
1984.
Stein, Gertrude. *The Autobiography of Alice B. Toklas.* New York:
Random House, 1960.
Street, Julian. *Where Paris Dines.* Garden City, N.Y.: Doubleday
Doran & Co., 1929.
Svoboda, Frederic Joseph. *Hemingway and The Sun Also Rises.*
Lawrence, Kansas: University Press of Kansas, 1983.
Tate, Allen. *Memoires and Opinions 1926–1974.* Chicago: Swallow
Press, 1975.
Thomson, Virgil. *Virgil Thomson.* New York: Alfred A. Knopf,
1966.

Warnod, André. *Bals, Cafés, & Cabarets*. Paris: E. Figuieure et Cie., 1913.

Wickes, George. *Americans in Paris*. New York: Doubleday & Company, 1969.

Williams, William Carlos. *The Autobiography of William Carlos Williams*. New York: Random House, 1951.

Wolff, Geoffrey. *Black Sun*. New York: Random House, 1976.

Woon, Basil. *The Paris that's not in the Guide Books*. New York: Brentano's, 1926.

THE PEOPLE OF HEMINGWAY'S PARIS

— An Annotated Index ——————————————————————

This index lists real people and fictional characters mentioned in the guide and walking tours. The accompanying descriptions are provided to jog readers' memories, and are in no way intended to be complete. Numbers in brackets indicate the number of the listing in the guide; page numbers in italics indicate a photograph.

THE PLACES OF HEMINGWAY'S PARIS

— An Index ——————————————————————————————

This index lists all places mentioned in the guide and walking tours. Numbers in brackets indicate the number of the listing in the guide; page numbers in italics indicate a photograph.